Jack's Beans

By the same author

poetry:

Spending the Light (Fithian Press, 2004)
Trash: the Dahmer Sonnets (Red Moon Press, 2000)
Cow'sleap: a Nightbook (Fithian Press, 1999)
Waiting on Pentecost (Birch Brook Press, 1999)
The Broken Iris (Persephone Press, 1991)
Traffic (The Smith Publishers, 1984)
Singing the Middle Ages (The Countryman Press, 1982)
Some Traffic (Beyond Baroque Foundation, 1976)

novel:

A Well-Behaved Little Boy (Woldt, 1993)

TOM SMITH

Jack's Beans

A Five Year Diary

For Laura —
Joy!

Tom Smith
9-12-06

BIRCH BROOK PRESS

First Edition
Library of Congress Control Number: 2006924866
ISBN: 9780913559970

Cover art by Anita Lobel

Published by
        Birch Brook Press
        PO Box 81
        Delhi, NY 13753

Write for a free catalog of books & art
birchbrookpress@usadatanet.net
Visit us at www.birchbrookpress.info

acknowledgments

The following periodicals have published pages, entries, or thematic sequences from this collection: *Beyond Baroque 793* (October 1979), *Lake Effect* (Spring 1990), *James White Review* (Summer 1993), *Beloit Poetry Journal* (Fall 1993), *Brussels Sprout* (September 1993), *Lynx* (February 1994), *Pemmican #3* and #4, *New Digressions* (Fall 1995), *Iowa Review* (Fall 1995), *New York Quarterly* (Spring 1996), *Pemmican #6* and #8 (1997 & 1999).

Remembering Arnold

"What we have loved
Others will love, and we will teach them how."
Wordsworth, *The Prelude* XIV, 446-7

"Some have accused me of a strange design..."
Byron, *Don Juan* IV, v

JANUARY 1

Beginning Again & Again

1950 Uncle Skunk. The TV
lurid, eerie in the darkened
parlor at midnight: Times Square.
Ten thousand strangers
make me wonder.
1951 "If all time's eternally present,"
I've an unnecessary ticket.
"Careful–if you breathe, it breaks!"
says Laura to her gentleman.
Ain't we dainty in our cricket cage?
1952 They have all come home from their colleges.
Miss Shrimp, for instance, hasn't changed,
only found new objects for her old contempt.
Denver has shed her inhibitions: *plashless*.
Hermes is acquiring authority. He has a girl.
1953 Order has no issue.
Greatness mutates in chaos.
This is what Rimbaud declares.
A soul must be hoodwinked: tedious,
sublime, & sensible derangement.
1954 Lilian violates my journal
while I'm on the john or running
after Viceroys at the corner. *Wrecks all?*
My heart is deceitful above all things
& meant for publication.

JANUARY 2

The Unshoveled Path

1950 I clerked this afternoon at County Public.
Leering Jane Beard accosted me, "Can't
imagine where you'll be in–say, ten years."
No one believes I can survive.
They can't, in fact, believe that I'm here now.
1951 On my way to Laura's New Year's Eve
I stumbled in the dark upon a dead
squirrel in the unshoveled path.
Coming home through falling snow
I trod the other side of the street.
1952 Reading U S history
for the Regents:
pilgrims & pioneers.
Flags & fools can't keep
my fist out of my pants.
1953 We are finished.
I should have eaten
his wings off.
Jackie, nibble
to the quick.
1954 She had no business in my book.
I dare not cite her prying.
She'd think me mad.
I'd only mean we're even.
Some gods feed on us daily.

JANUARY 3

Values

1950 *Red Hot & Blue* (B Hutton):
idiot determination wins stardom.
I believe hard work succeeds.
Friend Hermes says talent's a factor.
I'll be a writer in The City & have writer friends.
1951 A storm broods
always & everywhere
unspoken
but impressed upon our senses.
The sensitive mind expects it.
1952 "Who never thought
in terms of flags
and never served
a lesser loyalty
than humankind."
1953 Now I'm in Brooklyn with Sybil & Lew.
Hermes & easy Hot Fudge escort me
to plays & galleries.
Catholic Theresa
asks to see me Sunday morning.
1954 I encounter her bland eye.
"Your values?" She shrugs & shudders.
"My values ain't worth puzzling over, Lil."
She thinks I am Narcissus & obscene.
It's a howler.

JANUARY 4

Basilisk

1950 Spring session confirms delinquency.
High school wastes time.
I wonder how anyone can be happy.
I am sometimes happy: human beings
have great spirit & forgetfulness.
1951 "Mist and murk and lassitude
Darken air; surrender mood:"
Rolfe Humphries in a Fall *New Yorker*.
Wrote all night; finished short story.
Basilisk attacks me & takes hold.
1952 "Conservatives *and* liberals
take over government with zeal
convinced truth crushed
to earth has risen
again."
1953 She said she no longer loves Hermes.
Her family's intrusion confused
her internal conflict:
to be in love with Hermes;
not to be in love.
1954 A Brooklyn weekend:
I share a bed with Mr. Bear
& she flops out with Fudge.
Mock decorum.
Slapstick propriety.

JANUARY 5

O Rosary!

1950 A letter came to homeroom
from a Japanese student.
We sent books to his school
last fall. He thinks
we're all rich & happy.

1951 LIFE
IS
NOT
ART
IS

1952 "The desire
to continue
in power
encourages
timidity & compromise."

1953 Catholic Theresa.
What did she see in Hermes?
O Rosary! O Star of David!
She finds her own trained, arbitrary heart
still glowing in the dark: no exit.

1954 We inherit a shared despair
in the hot, eternal Pullman,
Half her checked baggage arrives.
No anger left. No tears. Her patience.
This dry horror of my soul.

JANUARY 6

A Hard Chair

1950 Sneak preview at Proctors
with Hermes. *The Hasty Heart*
(Pat Neal & Richard Todd).
Rain fell. The trees are in armor.
I envy nature.

1951 ART
IS
NOT
LIFE
IS

1952 "Liberals grow constantly
more liberal. Conservatives grow less
conservative. The process
is not only periodic
but progressive."

1953 Hermes stands stiff
& hoards himself, his hair
like a red sea.
I'd spill all over dirty
water like a wrung sponge.

1954 Dog shit on the kitchen floor.
Note, misspelled, from absent landlord.
I left my luggage in the hall,
sat on a hard chair until dawn,
found a pay phone: "Mom?"

JANUARY 7

Reversals

1950 Snow fell.
Drifts crowd the traffic.
Stalled trees
in lucite scabbards
stab bright eyes.
1951 Art
creates;
life
only
chances.
1952 It's clear
the process has reversed itself
in this dark decade.
Conservativae Cronos
devours each bright babe.
1953 Lew dubbed her The Palisades Princess
& cackled, "Crown her with a poker."
I wish he'd get his teeth fixed.
Sybil & Hot Fudge "exchanged glances."
I'd like to know what women mean by that.
1954 Slammed books & clothes & records
in the trunk & backseat while my dad
fussed about the paint job & upholstery.
I thank God for the paint job & upholstery.
Moma's clean house saves.

JANUARY 8

A Windblown Look

1950 The family can't read so why not write it
down: I have a lover & perhaps I am in love.
He stepped in the unbroken snow to let me pass.
I turned & he was catching up behind me.
I looked in a window at some dummies.
1951 Art finds
plan & meaning
& can give
meaning & plan
to life's muddle.
1952 Hermes has a girl
& I went down
to meet her.
Grand Central Station.
Stone flowers. Lions' manes.
1953 Hot Fudge really likes guys.
We were seated on the subway
& a strap-hanger
thrust us a bold sketch in taut pants.
"Don't you love a windblown look!" she yelled.
1954 Hunger for bear meat,
thirst for lily.
"Purity of heart
is to will one thing."
I cannot. I must.

JANUARY 9

Running on Air

1950 Spare me these cross
examinings."Moma,
I wasn't out *all* night."
Why am I such a waste of time?
Take me away, Joe, take me...

1951 Art
finds
&
can
give.

1952 Heretical Theresa.
Hermes' bloom
in the gloom
larks the lush dullness
of her Jesuit-rich rearing.

1953 Lew's on a rampage. A stark
apartment met us on the stair.
We found out Sybil on the Esplanade.
We wished on the lighted ferry,
blew it to Staten.

1954 Crumpled briefs under my desk chair.
Shiver & skip of Moma's Frigidaire.
There's my head on the ploughshare
pillow & the cat's damned stare.
O! Mr. Bear.

JANUARY 10

Hag Fate

1950 People who play safe
for Paradise are cowards:
won't live; won't let me
live my heart out & my brains.
Their fear unmakes Heaven.
1951 Similitude, design
bring me & bare me.
Art & experience,
interdepending,
not interchangeable.
1952 Hermes & Theresa take
their love seriously. Nothing is beautiful
until it is taken seriously & it is
beautiful only to those who are serious.
Their love is very beautiful.
1953 Lew was baking a cake
for our last evening in Brooklyn.
He drank the vanilla and blacked out.
Sailed home on a grey dawn
with his pants on backward.
1954 Hag Fate
has such
a dirty wit.
She has only
to wait.

JANUARY 11

He Means Me

1950 Perhaps there is a God. I'm sure there is.
I'm not sure he means well. I think he means
for me to make the most of Earth & the world.
I think he means me to be happy in my choices.
I think he means me to discover who I am.
1951 I have shut myself up in my room:
new yellow pads & pencils,
World Almanac & Book of Facts.
Something in that.
TV wrings the family through evening worship.
1952 Judith Anderson at City Center: *Come of Age.*
The movies: *Roshomon,* Menotti's *Medium.*
Dinner at 17 Barrow Street.
Three bloomin' kids
in a drizzle.
1953 My coat of many colors
is all holes. Once life was simple.
I whacked off. I had no past.
Jack Spider, weave.
Weave, Jack.
1954 Hermes writes to call me names.
I've nothing to hold onto but my guilt.
Moma flies her broom around the kitchen.
"Lift your feet."
I never meant to be a monster.

JANUARY 12

Mean to Make

1950 I mean to make my heaven here on earth.
I don't know that I'll have another chance.
To be happy is a duty, aim, & discipline.
To exercise my curiosity & joy. To practice
forgetfulness of insults & hostilities.
1951 Rejected poems
haul their tails home
from *Harper's*. Jesus,
I'd like it heavy & head on
under a fast truck or some rough trucker.
1952 Hermes has written: "Theresa
declares you a Michelangelo.
Hail! Heroic Spirit!
Lustrous Anarch!"
Demon. Demon.
1953 Lilian & Dixie & I
dawdled at coffee
after our Lit Final.
Then Bluejay stood behind me
bundling his peacoat around my ears.
1954 A monster
& dumb.
Dumb because
Mr. Bear
don't care.

JANUARY 13

"Gotcha, Ferdinand!"

1950 My instinct is retreat.
The world is a crashing bully.
I'm only a fairy flower
brimming with secret & sweet
poisons: "Gotcha, Ferdinand!"
1951 Saturday mornings are slow at County Public.
I hide in the stacks with Andre Gide,
The Diary of Adam by Mark Twain,
Nijinsky, Isadora Duncan,
Letters of Hart Crane.
1952 It's curious how Christopher & Laura
have sought each other out for battle.
Only wit & quibble
until this afternoon at the Plaza.
Poor show: mostly Laura's ass.
1953 Alex North's *Streetcar*
grinding off the phonograph,
I worked up a phantom Bluejay.
The music filled me
& my cup ran over.
1954 I always seem to be flung back on some dump.
Patchwork Jack
& spanking new,
life ain't hardly
done with you.

JANUARY 14

Down for the Count

1950 The whole town swoons nightly from ten to twelve
for Joe the whispering DJ who found me in the snow.
I'm the wayward JD with the key to his apartment.
"Cole Porter wraps it up from station WOW.
Murphy, you'd be so nice to come home to."
1951 Laura has Welkin helping her write a speech
for some contest. He invited her home
& burned a steak.
She talks too much
& he's, of course, polite.
1952 I'm getting superstitious about threes.
I count to ten
over Christopher or Laura;
divide the gloom
with Sybil over Lew.
1953 Hermes will be home.
I want him to meet Lilian & Dixie.
Lilian's a friend.
I let her read my novel.
I like her height: Big Blonde.
1954 Exams won't be taxing.
I have a little time
to work my prose poems (*First Hand*);
to start my novel
(*Spring Came on Forever*).

JANUARY 15

A Murphy Stew

1950 Murphy's the bed
& swings out of a closet.
We share a snack
& put another nickel in
Theresa Brewer.
1951 Welkin's apartment, says Laura, is mostly ash-
trays. Apple parings, orange peels, & butts. Bed
spread with newspapers & science fiction. Pulp.
I hung around his classroom until five.
They worked. I watched out the window.
1952 Chris is his own scarecrow.
I slip him blue notes between classes.
"Conformity's the sin against the Holy Ghost.
Thought you should know."
He rips into Boys with a royal flush.
1953 Dixie falls on the crowd
in a mechanic's coverall
with earrings & spike heels.
"I want a man."
She slips a finger down my throat.
1954 I have thrown myself into the task.
First Hand must have a preface.
The novel waits.
The family ignore me.
I'm invisible.

JANUARY 16

Damp Panics

1950 Frank Sinatra & Gene Kelly *On the Town*.
Cute is a sailor suit. "I died for beauty."
Emily Dickinson. Dark as the movies
or a grave (with technicolor at one's toes)
or my damp panic in a crowd.
1951 We are reading *The East* in Senior English.
Buddha returning love for hatred. Haiku by Buson,
Basho. Chinese Tu Fu, Li Po, T'ung Han-Ching.
Kao-Shih (Golden Age of the Tang Emperors): "Down
the streets of old Liang/Old echoes wail and die."
1952 I don't like what's happening to Laura.
Total recall & perfect incomprehension.
Loud talk! Loud laughter! break the tension.
Then she faints. Determined to subordinate
her genius to parents & peers.
1953 Some girls (Hot Fudge for instance)
meet me head on.
That's how it is with Dixie.
Sex is one thing. Poetry's another.
We're both whores. But she is not a poet.
1954 Mystery of automatic writing.
Every moment rings
the very thing.
The sea-nymphs'
ding-dong-ding.

JANUARY 17

Behind the Comics

1950 Her neighbor died for truth.
It's been killing me
ever since Candyland's Long John
filled my sugar cone
behind the comics.
1951 *Ida A Novel* by Gertrude Stein.
I've heard her mocked.
The mockery did make me curious.
They call her *avant garde*.
I find her quaint.
1952 The world is killing her.
She gives over with both hands
trembling with fear & rage.
Her brain is pure murder
& would hack out of this madhouse.
1953 She sails onstage,
the person in the play,
the author's vessel.
Now we're solid
caterpillar: butterfly.
1954 "Full Fathom Five" sounds
the deep, the deepest
lyric ever sung.
At last: I know
what I'm doing.

JANUARY 18

Crumbs

1950 My own lies
master me
like weeds, choke me
out of the garden.
Who am I? Where am I?
1951 I AM I:
This symmetry
recurs through *Ida*
becoming an emblem.
Malevich's *White on White*.
1952 Full of rumor!
The whole school audits us.
We're fable. It's terror.
I'm reading her pages of *Dorian Gray*
& she can not shut up.
1953 Our film club presented *Camille*.
I had never seen Greta Garbo.
She is *unlike*. . .
I could not have anticipated
beauty that is genius realized.
1954 I'm following
Hansel's cake crumbs
through the woods
& I'm one step ahead
of the birds.

JANUARY 19

Crashing through Hedges

1950 I'm 16. Troubled about sex?
  Only the hiding
  cheapens our affair.
  I want to be honest.
  Mom & Dad won't hear.
1951 Doors & windows seem organic.
  Not personification:
  the life is their own.
  The words rise up:
  an insurrection of toy soldiers.
1952 "Get back to your bugs."
  I have seen her happy
  in the field
  with net & sturdy shoes
  or meditating on a mounted beetle.
1953 How to write about Lilian?
  I keep no secrets.
  I don't camp.
  In her company
  I'm Gentleman Jack.
1954 Morris crashing through a hedge
  in prose slow motion. Welkin
  melting into his Bourbon. Laura
  leaving me: Monarch
  crossing Atlantic.

JANUARY 20

Chasing Rabbits

1950 I can't remember when
  I've not resented
  the drab facts
  & resorted
  to fancies, fantasies, fables, lies.
1951 "That is really why they danced
  in the moonlight they thought
  they were chasing rabbits any shadow
  was a rabbit to them"—Stein
  about a family of hounds.
1952 Laura collector. Laura entomologist.
  We must think things
  like art & insects
  & let God think people.
  He can handle it. Maybe.
1953 Hermes at home between semesters.
  Dixie whipped the winter afternoon
  with wit & cigarettes. Lilian: plump
  & stately at a meal & the movies.
  Bluejay? Gone south I guess.
1954 Rimbaud provides a serpent sheen:
  "We were two
  good children
  free to wander
  in a paradise of sorrows."

JANUARY 21

The Real Dope

1950 Imagine on a bike
tailing California plates
convinced a scout would zip me off to Hollywood.
What was I peddling?
The songs & dances of my daydreams.
1951 Mother loves not
Ida. I haven't
seen her so
outraged & afraid
since she caught me with *The City and the Pillar.*
1952 Monarch & mimic Viceroy. Luna
moth & Ghost. Jack with wings.
The powder rubs off
on your inexpert fingers
& makes you sneeze.
1953 Self-love keeps faith
a true world lies inside
but ego is in love
with making a good impression.
It is faithless & afraid of the self.
1954 Welkin staggers to the bright conclusion
that his one bright student is a fairy.
Where is he now? The real dope.
I think I'll have him burn down
in a stupor as drunks do.

JANUARY 22

That's the Ticket

1950 Falsehood comes home.
I am resolved to be truthful
as far as friends allow.
I'll have these pages
practice a truthful habit.
1951 Laura has forced my farce to an abrupt curtain:
last laugh dying away in the stable.
She couldn't take my vapors any longer.
She laid my crush open.
Welkin's "got no taste for it."
1952 Lew marched our tickets into the library.
City Center's Sunday matinee.
Swan Lake, Ravel's *La Valse*,
Robbins' *Ballade* to Debussy.
We will be joined by Hermes & his lady.
1953 I'm not opposed to objectivity.
I even suppose it's possible.
But the fabric
& to some extent the craft
come from the inward person.
1954 Where's Laura? At Cornell
majoring in something agricultural.
She's taken a farmer beau & joined a church.
Seems to have made up her mind
about everything.

JANUARY 23

Double Exposure

1950 Early to bed is good for Mom & Dad.
Their snores wash me out the backdoor.
Snow squeaks under my feet & old trees
rattle. His apartment warms & radio
whispers me off my mackinaw & foolish heart.
1951 "That Welkin's the limit!" said Denver
& Laura slid me a glance.
Somebody shouted *swell* down the hall.
I'm indifferent & wonder
why I plod such banal plots.
1952 Lew borrowed a camera & shot us.
The best is an accident:
her head, a great rose on her nape,
sails in profile over my full face.
Our lips exactly meet.
1953 Errors & illusions:
old skins to be shed
with delicate attention
for they hint
the essential shape.
1954 The keys perform their little vaudeville
beneath my fingers. Claptrap extensions
of my brain. The pages sing.
Since I've messed up every other matter,
let me exult in this competence.

JANUARY 24

Policed by Joy

1950 I do not understand how other people
judge or why they must police my joy.
I, meanwhile, induced
blue-rinsed Miss Blazes
to teach our history class the Charleston.
1951 Three worlds: the body
(it aint what it seems);
the intellect (gluttonous brain);
the spirit (unique
pigeon).
1952 O see the uneasy pilgrims
push through a promising snowfall
overtown to see Cocteau.
Beauty and the Beast.
We went together & we all came home alone.
1953 Should a man achieve perfect objectivity,
he'd stand apart in his attainment.
Outwardness, however, rests in common sense.
Should I, however, fathom my own soul,
I'd have a whole world only I can know.
1954 Miss Shrimp attacks Morris with a bottle
& he passes out. Dissolve
to brief infinity. Imagine her
going into nursing.
Maybe life is strange enough.

JANUARY 25

Tricks of Light

1950 My convictions
alter my appearance:
a trick of light.
Pleasure absorbs
more luminous refractions.
1951 My body? My mind? My spirit?
Nothing knows nothing.
Perception is
prejudice learning
error upon error.
1952 Laura provides
the facts & I compose
a decade of poems
about butterflies.
A birthday suite.
1953 Hermes refuses to mourn.
"Living through it was enough.
There's work to do
& other women in the world."
He drives me crazy.
1954 Writing is a space craft.
I'm the tic on old Luna.
Necessary isolation heals.
I aim my time machine at touchdown.
Regeneration A: BC.

JANUARY 26

The Object Subject

1950 This object
of jibes & jests
has not escaped
unconscious
as a bug.
1951 Perception becomes reality.
The mask I show
the world becomes
the mask I see.
I call it *me*.
1952 The train will be heat & horsehair.
I will comfort myself
with *The Importance of Being Earnest.*
Also *Oscar Wilde* by Andre Gide.
Sybil will bring marascas in gin.
1953 "It moves me."
The work is edifice
not outhouse.
Poetry only begins in motion.
It ends in rest.
1954 I crash through Moma's rooms
clutching a manuscript sandwich,
grinding my pretty
retractible teeth,
slavering syllables.

JANUARY 27

The Whack & Bite of Body

1950 Self-glorifying leap into the soul of space!
What do I mean?
I am an urge
to talk back
at the world.
1951 Relieve me of this body.
I might be happy
as an observant spirit
with crayons
& lots of blank clouds.
1952 We sucked the last cherries
from slim bottles on the steps
of Saint Patrick. We teased
brash Atlas Aloft. We lunched
with Hermes & Theresa at the Russian Tearoom.
1953 Split a Burgundy with Hermes
who returns to his spring semester.
At last he put words to his fear.
"Life, I don't think, will come to me."
I offered. But he shied away.
1954 *First Hand* is assembled.
Impeccably typed.
O! MS!
Everything comes
to black on white.

JANUARY 28

Knock Knock

1950 My Saturday morning stint at County Public
leaves me ravenous. I slide downhill to Riverside.
Joe has prepared a table.
We blow kisses across hot spoons.
Murphy purrs in the corner.
1951 I will never be easy in my body.
Too many other bodies knock
about me. What alerts
their bloody gorgeosity
to my pale emptiness?
1952 How urgently
I needed Lew & Sybil to adore
Theresa! She must find them brilliant.
I will be the center
of a dazzling company.
1953 Rhythms
pulse from some core of mystery.
What is their content?
Have I a personal webster?
What causes loom in me?
1954 Fled the house.
It seemed an awful chicken
in some Russian fairy tale.
I hung out at Greyhound
ducking the vice squad.

JANUARY 29

Some Strangers on a Raft

1950 Before Joe was Rasputin,
clerk in Records & Periodicals;
Ray, my rum & Coca Cola daddy;
some strangers on a raft;
some kids who shared a budding.
1951 I have finished my fable of Henry
who lives in a big house on a wide lawn.
His children grow up. His wife dies.
He buys two hundred trees & plants them.
Then he goes inside & waits.
1952 Savage Ravel
left me mute
in my seat
& the dancers
took me apart.
1953 I died one summer day six months ago.
The morning Hermes started on my portrait.
I saw all thought & spirit depart.
I cite no cause of death. Nothing befell
except the nature of the animal.
1954 I should call Lilian.
We can make a new beginning.
Why this
vacuous
haunting of public places?

JANUARY 30

Broad Face

1950 Rasputin wanted only hugs
among the dead Gazettes & Stars.
When I invited him to sup,
he called me
a bad name.
1951 As I was reading shelves
a boy appeared beside me.
Backward.
The broad face
hanging askance of my smile.
1952 Mused through the late afternoon
over Laura's collection
while she lectured.
She carpenters the little box frames
& prints the India labels perfectly.
1953 One day or another the corpse has stirred.
Now an incongruous season
burgeons inside me.
My body trembles.
Brains & blood are running.
1954 Dumb. Dumb. Dumb. Dumb.
Dull. Dumb. Dumb. Dumb.
Dull. Dull. Dumb. Dumb.
Dull. Dull. Dull. Dumb.
Dumb. Dumb. Dumb. Dumbbell.

JANUARY 31

Toward Holy Land

1950 Joe loves me very well, but grown men will
stop short of some fulfillment. He'd rather thrill
my head with grues: "It'll give you cancer."
This child of sighs
doesn't care how he dies.

1951 A common carrot-top,
his head rolled & he gaped
at the ceiling while he asked,
"What're ya doing?"
Every idiot asks that.

1952 The fritillaries are named for a kind of lily.
Checkered blossom. Speckled wing.
Coincidence is not design.
They live by sucking nectar & like me
prefer thistles & brambles.

1953 Hermes dreamed
I was sailing to Europe
in a rowboat.
The waters run
toward Holy Land.

1954 I broke one novel
into Moma's largest pot.
Fed all my fancies to the match.
Now a charred circle
mars her kitchen table.

FEBRUARY 1

Jumping Jack

1950 My little buddies in a shed or up
   the old appletree behind the A&P were far
   more perverted than big lovers are.
   We were more playful, less intent
   on the winnowing spasm.
1951 I opened a picture book
   of Washington DC.
   At every monument
   he pointed:
   "That's a far jump."
1952 The larva's
   protrusible osmeterium,
   normally hidden,
   can be suddenly erected.
   Even Apollo has one.
1953 I move into myself.
   Rhythms of life.
   Rhythms of my life.
   Spirited interplay
   of sound & sounding board.
1954 "It's a wonder
   you didn't burn the house down,"
   frets Moma.
   A fine leap free
   of old trash.

FEBRUARY 2

Pulling Together

1950 We protracted a foreplay
through seven summers pulling
together toward that first ejaculation spilled
into some mother's immaculate
bathroom sink.
1951 His older brother
stamped a foot
at the end of the aisle.
Then, taking his alien
by the hand, looked back.
1952 Taxonomy: Psyche, Apollo, Nymph,
Lysander, Lunus, Junonia, Helicon.
Morphoi. Hesperi. Satyridae.
Brimstone & Sulphur science
would be mute without mythology.
1953 Life is a music.
Friends & lovers
are harmonies
reflecting me.
Reflect upon them.
1954 Lilian remarks about branded
coldcuts from the supermarket,
make-believe meats
smothered in plastic wrap,
"They taste like tears."

FEBRUARY 3

Perhaps They Are Me

1950 Trees grope the wind.
  The grass sleeps off
  last summer's madcap.
  Fear not.
  We need nothing.
1951 It was a visitation:
  idiot boy & gentle brother's rage.
  They are perhaps one person.
  Perhaps they are me.
  Maybe the three of us are someone else.
1952 When Lady Glanville in the eighteenth century
  died, her disappointed heirs contested her will,
  maintaining she was clearly mad for she collected
  butterflies. The court declared:
  curiosity is sane. Even in women.
1953 Circulation of my blood.
  Phases of the moon. Ingestion.
  Digestion. Excretion. Seasons. Years.
  Bluejay at the bookstore
  rang up my spring texts.
1954 Classes resumed yesterday.
  Hang on the institutional patterns.
  Nothing from Mr. Bear. Nothing from Sybil & Lew.
  So stripped of identity
  everyone's a stranger.

FEBRUARY 4

What the Wind Said

1950 "Live," says the wind.
My heart says yes.
"Ponder." Yes. "Give & take."
"Lo!" Yes, for look & love.
"Behold!" Be whole & all.
1951 Welkin addressed me at work. We conducted
awkward discussion of Will Shakespeare. We might
have found a point to turn personal but Shrimp
charged in. "A great while ago the world began,"
sings the clown. "With hey, ho, &c."
1952 Pigmentation of the common white
derives from leucopterine,
chemical substance
formerly confused
with uric acid.
1953 Bluejay, unbreakfasted with patches
of toilet paper on his throat & chin,
stood by my commuter's locker.
"You & your Queen Anne's Lace,"
I said. He didn't understand.
1954 Lilian will go home to Long Island.
She wants to fetch
her Henry J.
She wants to leave me
on my own in Brooklyn.

FEBRUARY 5

Warning Coloration

1950 My prettiness
invites lust:
admiration & abuse.
I inherit
the world's ambivalence.
1951 "Some shall be pardon'd, and some punished."
Prince, I do not believe it.
Some live, some lie.
"Never was a story of more woe."
The wind & the rain.
1952 Camouflage is not the only way.
Monarchs survive by warning coloration,
wear their poison gaily as a caution.
Cardenolide:
bad for the heart & tummy.
1953 Then there's the cotton plugging
a morbid stench in his left ear.
What do I care? Why have I moped?
There's only one love story,
one dull way to play it.
1954 Together on the train
like dice in a box.
One thought between us
splits like an amoeba
as we part.

FEBRUARY 6

Say Boo

1950 If God or the gods
gave us minds & bodies,
gave us each other,
for salvation,
do they weep at our broken usage?
1951 If naturalism is the proper content
& normalcy the right criterion of style,
how is Will our greatest poet?
He is all dreams, riddles & nonsense.
His sympathy finds no norm, his curiosity no nature.
1952 Bowwow pursued me into Gentlemen's
at County P&, having made a proud
display of his intentions, asked
if he might take me to a movie.
"I'm crazy for movies!"
1953 He promises he's grown
during these months.
I groan,
but I'll waft on the wind of whatever
spook says boo.
1954 Sat up all night with Hot Fudge
who listened to my woes,
my self-recriminations,
resolutions.
She shrugs it all off.

FEBRUARY 7

Some Empty Places

1950 Ethel Waters'
black tide
rafts me down
the moody solution
of her tragicomic presence.
1951 Words rush off my feelings
with such force & sudden utterance
I am too apt to accept their truth.
Resonance often signifies
an empty place.
1952 He took me
to *The Devil*
in the Flesh,
the Zanzibar,
some terrible hotel.
1953 Romance makes me an object.
Potter's wheel.
I reel
& rise round
the ideal shaft.
1954 Hot fudge sprawls on a rented sofa.
Matisse goddess: cumulonimbus.
Yawns & says, "Life
is a nice girl. Always ready
to slap your face."

FEBRUARY 8

The Dog's World

1950 How do a free people
express themselves?
A naked song?
A dance in the streets?
Wouldn't worry me!
1951 When I am happy, pain has never been.
When I am sad, earth is a ball of dirt.
The world's a beetle.
Jack of Hearts
describes the looking-glass.
1952 He is really a very good Bowwow.
Healthy. All shots.
Housebroken to a widowed mother.
Good appetite.
Fond of children.
1953 Human beings are not limited to rut.
Maybe that is why we complicate
the fact of sex with every sort
of conventional fuss & fury:
tails tolled by a romantic idiot.
1954 Lew & Sybil dote.
Everybody's friend,
Hermes takes all sides. Mr. Bear
has bronchitis & the crabs.
A perfect weekend.

FEBRUARY 9

Accountings

1950 Class discussion: *Merchant of Venice*.
Shylock's Jewishness accounts for his behavior.
Nobody knows what Portia means by mercy.
Judge not?
What fool or communist said that?
1951 My need looks too much after answers.
Only the absolute
dismissal or panacea
is acceptable.
What is the question?
1952 I'm counting syllables for *Butterflies*
in the manner of the Japanese
& Miss Marianne Moore.
This puts me in a new relation to the words.
I whittle on stilts.
1953 We knock about the lockers,
tell the janitor
we couldn't find the light.
How seriously ordinary people go about
the business of guarding my morals!
1954 Driving upstate with Henry J,
climbing the globe into an upper bunk.
It's history's first Sunday all the way
& we're singing the old songs
of our innocence.

FEBRUARY 10

The Groundhog's Ditty

1950 Women,
  Jews, Negroes,
  Communists,
  cripples & freaks,
  Jack Bean.
1951 Deadlines.
  Deadlines,
  for instance,
  horrify me
  to defiance.
1952 My butterflies
  are made in art
  as they grow in nature.
  Process is as fine as finish.
  The reader should feel it.
1953 He was fighting me,
  fighting his nature.
  The struggle exhausts.
  The giant feeds. "Fee! Fie!"
  Ho hum.
1954 Spring semester. Keep faith
  & look away from the shadows.
  We are groundhogs here,
  our snackbar & lounges
  subterranean.

FEBRUARY 11

Morbid Resources

1950 Since kindergarten
mockery has been my daily bread.
The trembling thing expects it.
Morbid resources of fierce pride
engorge me. I am a person.

1951 I have seen one corpse.
A neighborhood elder displayed among flowers.
My mother led me in.
She knelt & signed herself & prayed.
I knelt & signed myself & prayed.

1952 His prettiness, dear friend, is tough
& not for the birds as
birds learn soon enough. Cas-
ual, brave parade of unruf-
fled wit drifting topaz!

1953 Acceptance turns
the enemy away. He grows
smaller & more transparent as he goes.
He falls off the horizon.

1954 The campus is a goddamned allegory. Student
activities, provisions for the body's needs take
space in cellar rooms & tunnels. Administrators
function at street level. Classrooms & faculty
offices soar second & third-storied Ariel!

FEBRUARY 12

Private Property

1950 A neighbor brat sasses an old scold,
"It's a free country."
The elder replies, "It is not.
It is a capitalist nation
& this is private property."
1951 When I was a toddler
I loved to bury stones,
bottle caps, broken toys, my socks.
Once I laid every stitch to rest
in a corner lot & strode home naked.
1952 Four-six-eight: appreciable pat-
terns flutter to take shape
on the page: ticks or tape-
worm eggs maze & mottle the flat
white pulp: alphabet ape.
1953 Required history & science.
Public speaking. French.
Electives: modern poetry,
survey of American painting,
romanticism in philosophy.
1954 The staff of the college
magazine convened last night.
I met the editor & his gang.
They think past issues
have lacked mass appeal.

FEBRUARY 13

Gloria Mundi

1950 A bishop once in Poland told my grampa
the walks of Hell
are paved with priests.
Suddenly Moma's
herding me to church.
1951 Graduation hurries near. I fail
to find a niche among the living.
Nine-to-five & a payday.
Everyone will notice
I do not belong.
1952 Tomorrow will be Laura's birth-
day & the valentine
done. The swallowtail sign
says keep courage as mute as earth
& mirthfully salt mine.
1953 Student commuter.
Sic transit omnibus.
I'm a slow reader.
I'm a fast talker.
Combustible Lucifer.
1954 Yes, mass appeal.
Fat strippers have it.
Or you buy it
at drugstores, wear it
like a rainhat.

FEBRUARY 14

Of Wheels & Wings

1950 Since God is common as dirt
or dandelion wheels, I doubt
denominational possession of the Word.
Division oppresses the spirit.
Dogma shuts the gate.
1951 I'm not afraid of death.
Life has more terrors & I do not want.
I'm 17. Full of doing,
full of waiting,
full of dread.
1952 Laura enchanted
waved the pages
from both hands
aloft like wings
of cabbages.
1953 I'm a student & that's something.
I'm not apochryphal.
I make. I do. I know.
I can swing with Bluejay
on his perilous sunflower.
1954 After returning Lilian to her dorm
I shot downtown & found
Lollipop at Barcelona.
Virtue stands simple & at hand.
Why can't I withstand?

FEBRUARY 15

Eternal Locker Room

1950 Thoughtless obedience tones
no pilgrim. Ritual observance hones
no soldier. The soul
at Armageddon can't afford
the flab of a great church.
1951 The draft also may kill.
Eternal locker room & host
of first-class, private jocks
all jeering, jabbering.
"Jacqueline!"
1952 Bowwow shows me off in public places,
pays my way, conducts me among tables,
down aisles. He does the honors
with my seat & wrap.
Brings me home to meet his mother.
1953 Bluejay complains
attention I provoke
unnerves him.
It unnerves me too
I tell him. He looks puzzled.
1954 I consented
to be raped.
I filthify myself,
which nastiness defiles the world.
Defiles? Defies? 'Ere's the 'ell of it!

FEBRUARY 16

God is a Beautiful Baffle

1950 Moma worships cleaning house.
Dad worships doing nothing.
My religion wonders, ponders
beyond my little learning.
God is a beautiful baffle.
1951 Death romances,
oppresses, obsesses,
fascinates.
Think on the gentleman.
Think on the fly.
1952 Joe & a handful
kept me in a pumpkin,
our couplings unutterable.
Bowwow brings me smack
into the world.
1953 Sticks & stones
might break my bones.
"You certainly ask for it."
No one has to give me
what I ask for.
1954 Embattled
Jack stalks
the bean.
The bean
stalks Jack.

FEBRUARY 17

Necessary Angels

1950 Hermes alone
audits
my diary.
He becomes
its standard.
1951 The gentleman was death. The fly,
who buzzed, sums up the business
of the world. "I have been half
in love with easeful death,
with Beauty who must die."
1952 "You've been
a closet queen."
Sir Throne,
I have looked
at the cat.
1953 Wallace Stevens.
The Blue Guitar.
The Necessary Angel.
Essential light.
Language must equal its object.
1954 Never a new day.
The butterfly
remains
a worm
when you look right at it.

FEBRUARY 18

Centering Down

1950 Mr. Truman Capote
Shuts a Final Door:
all circles center down.
I think about bedsprings
& bottomless pits.
1951 Perhaps I spent too much
of my childhood romping
in a graveyard. We used
to strip among the stones.
"The yanks are coming."
1952 He dubbed me
Sweet Bitch.
Oxymoron!
Never thought I'd encounter
such figures in real life.
1953 Imperative!
Imperative's another habit
I can't break:
sun must feed,
moon must fatten.
1954 *Desire nothing* says the stoic.
I hate his righteousness and beg
Lilian to have mercy
& patience while I trim
desire at her shrine.

FEBRUARY 19

I Am Not the Person Who Got Hurt

1950 Hermes says I should acquire
facts. I ordered a subscription
to *Writer's Digest*.
Flair by Fleur arrives
at all the downtown newsstands.
1951 In Saint Panther's Cemetery
Ray first had me
under some ginkgos & a granite
finger pointing at Heaven
while his spaniels ran loose.
1952 Wheel me out
to the center
ring. I'll stand
on my hindlegs
singing Bowwow.
1953 The people I meet are not
the people who have hurt me.
I am not the person who got hurt.
You're nobody I know.
I'm nobody you know.
1954 Soren Kierkegaard,
Purity of Heart
Is to Will One Thing.
I will myself to Lilian.
I'll meet her stately measure.

FEBRUARY 20

Guide Lines

1950 At Hermes' what breaks
gets fixed. My Dad snoozes.
Moma dusts a blown bulb.
Who cares about function?
I'm their child.
1951 Andre Gide is dead.
I was reading
Chinese pornography.
Moma announced behind her newspaper,
"Another writer died."
1952 Bowwow's crowd includes
Lollipop, Mortimer, Timothy,
& the Texans: Mash & Rex.
I absorb their glamour
sharing a snow-globe world.
1953 Boredom is the original sin.
Only mediocre people have opinions.
Some cannot live by ideals, others by illusions;
if you can't live up to either, you're a realist.
Epigrams assume an absurd authority.
1954 *Everybody's Autobiography.*
The Heel of Elohim.
The Web and The Rock.
A wolf. A wagoner.
A mug.

FEBRUARY 21

Elephants in Albany

1950 *Taboo* sounds a silly deep
& *Tabetha's* a witch's cat:
familiar *Tabby.*
Tibia toodles me *Tiber,*
Tiberius, Tub, & *Tibet.*
1951 Two Andres, Gide & Maurois.
One died. The other explained
Sartre at the college chapel.
Existentialism.
"Man is a will."
1952 Lollipop at home:
a pitcher of Manhattans.
Under a tea cozy:
the werewolf.
"Our man in the moons."
1953 Presumption is the spiritual form of epigram:
To approach a great book with boredom is immoral,
to leave it anything but humbled, a misfortune;
I dread the lovers of ideas
who think they are lovers of art.
1954 We went to the movies:
Alec Guinness in *The Captain's Paradise.*
Caught a bus to escape an immanent ice age.
On Lake Street at Washington two elephants
waited for the light.

FEBRUARY 22

A Quixote Syndrome

1950 The world won't be
my fortress
or my fare.
I want to see
a rain of clowns.
1951 "Man is a will. He's not an object:
beast or tree or rock. He is a subject.
Within him boils a world."
I must invent ideals,
morals, roses, windmills.
1952 Mortimer is invisible
with jowls & emits
a perpetual woof.
He's a bassett
swinging on a rainbow.
1953 One must always behave unintelligently;
how else can he learn from experience?
The satirical epigram slyly
holds up its own presumption
to ridicule.
1954 The circus is in town
but I don't think
I'll run away.
I don't like animals.
I'm bored by destiny.

FEBRUARY 23

The Grated Cheese

1950 Will I be able
   to imagine a clown
   without a broken heart?
   Have I capacity to strike
   beyond banality?
1951 Some advise me, "Be natural."
   They mean conform.
   Some rant, "Be realistic."
   A living means only
   a daily wage.
1952 Timothy is black Italian,
   blue-eyed Irish.
   Genes! O jeans!
   If only he wouldn't talk:
   boiled cabbage, grated cheese.
1953 Puritanism is the beginning of all great lusts.
   The true lovers of life are those who throw it away
   most thoughtfully. The only loss
   worth losing is
   one's soul.
1954 I ran away once when I was a kid.
   I stole a skirt & babushka from Pandora,
   changed clothes in Saint Panther's,
   started for New York City.
   A trucker offered me a ride.

FEBRUARY 24

A Great Many Persons & Places

1950 "O rare Ben Jonson." Burden
interrupted our class drift
to explain the famous epitaph
which may or may not pun:
orare is Latin *praise* or *pray for*.
1951 *Atlantic Monthly* (November 1950).
Agnes De Mille quotes Martha Graham:
"Ballet is largely poses,
linked with the lightest movement.
It strives to conceal effort."
1952 The Texans, in town
less than a year, preside.
Their apartment is Rome:
everyone comes
& anything goes.
1953 Ethel, editor
of the college news,
asked me to do a column.
I promised her,
"Something Wilde."
1954 Pandora blazed the dark
side of my childhood.
We sat on a stoop.
Behind a comic book, she'd grope
fetching out hot little hope.

Becoming Too Real

1950 My little Latin translates *oro*:
say Ben Jonson. Say Jack Boot.
I wonder why the old Hebrews
made God's name taboo.
Would he become too real in everybody's mouth?
1951 "Graham thought that effort
was life and using the ground,
rather than escaping it, was vital;
impulses flow through the body
as motion is sent through a whip."
1952 Rex, scientist & alcoholic,
doesn't drink.
He wanders
among the party
seeking an intelligent conversation.
1953 Sincerety is a fine art of rudeness.
We are never so pointless as to say what we mean.
Genius is more easily ignored than measured.
The measure of genius is its uselessness
to blockheads & workers.
1954 Pandora was one of history's
great masturbators. Once
we staged a battle
tearing each other's hair out:
handsful & roots.

FEBRUARY 26

The Vicar

1950 The human event
stands at a remove.
Life is vicarious.
Movies, novels, poems, paintings, songs
appropriate reality.
1951 "Thighs and knees
hinge the body
to the floor,
incorporate
the ground."
1952 Mash & Rex have been married nine years.
Mash is unfaithful
& fast & frankly lewd.
The quick fox trots.
Rex is a Buddhist.
1953 Epigrams for Ethel.
"Outrageous!" Yes,
it is absurd to be absolute.
Certainty is an attribute of language,
not of mind.
1954 *Six Characters*
in Search of an Author.
Somehow Shakespeare
started everything
with *Hamlet*.

FEBRUARY 27

The Fly

1950 Life is vicarious
   until I sharpen words,
   string *Beans*.
   On words I have sickened.
   Words will make me well.
1951 "When I had some success
   I went back to her and said,
   'There is no contentment.
   I see only faults.
   I get sick with dismay."
1952 The Buddhist looks for nothing.
   Mash takes advantage.
   The spider dances
   & the fly
   also dances.
1953 A letter from Theresa
   putting life together on a campus
   "sedate and almost sedative" in Virginia.
   She is close to Washington DC
   where the museums "are so perfectly established."
1954 I try to be
   the author of my existence.
   I imitate art & that
   is why it all comes out
   so vulgar & old hat.

FEBRUARY 28

"If That There King Was to Wake"

1950 An old blue mirror
  smokes my hanging face.
  Small star glitters beside my ear.
  My seeing it proves nothing.
  But a dream means someone sleeping.
1951 "There is only
  divine unrest.
  It is our privilege
  to know it,"
  said Martha G.
1952 He took me home
  to meet his mother.
  Proper bitch.
  No one ever threw her
  to the dogs.
1953 Theresa,
  I never felt
  the seed
  or sower.
  Here I am.
1954 I burden Lilian
  with the whole of my mind
  as I used to do Laura.
  Still girls keep silence!
  What are they waiting for?

MARCH 1

Stagecraft & Ethics

1950 My webster tangles
with *existentialism:*
"personal decision
in the face
of a universe without purpose."
1951 "Every young artist
needs a wall
to grow against
like a vine."
To grow *against.*
1952 When *elegant* Theresa
declares me *elegant,*
I wonder who I am.
Weeds are sometimes pretty.
Then they sprawl.
1953 My dear Theresa,
simplicity does not hoard;
it gathers not.
Here's my new poem:
"Baby, Baby, Born to Shooting"
1954 Shakespeare, British
Survey (Pope
to Present),
Modern Drama,
Stagecraft & Ethics.

MARCH 2

The Subject Object

1950 My choices
  are determined by forces
  that have no intentions.
  Am I not random
  & chance?
1951 I am a fierce urge
  to tell all. World,
  I want to be
  your erupted peony.
  Ants will invade.
1952 Trembling hands. Hesitation
  entering rooms, answering
  questions. Shivering breath.
  My symptoms, Theresa says, express
  an exquisite person.
1953 Stars like Betty Grable whose/ blue-lidded/ lustre
  sped/ spinning a spangled cosmos/ through my blood.
  Glittering flooz-/ ies floated (stanza)/ to the surface.
  Maureen O/ Sullivan/ taught Tarzan/ the words. I was
  nursed and toi-/ let trained in Girls' at the lo-/ cal Loews.
1954 Tiger boarded at the Capitol,
  sat down beside me.
  "What do you make of it?"
  he inquired of my Gertrude.
  With a twang.

MARCH 3

Mouse & Unicorn

1950 Nature & Art
   is all. Society
   doesn't matter.
   I should drift
   like stardust.
1951 I propose an ideal
   of love, but I cannot
   love everybody.
   I'm too selfish to love people
   when they're mean.
1952 For *mouse*
   read *unicorn?*
   I know I go masked.
   "Who's there?"
   "Nay, answer me. Stand and unfold yourself."
1953 Pan- (stanza)/ demonion sound tracked my/ brain.
   Each gan-/ glion sang/ Garland, Hayworth, Montez. I-/
   da Lupino. Myrna Loy./ Yes--"Bangbang!" (stanza)/ in
   backyard games, gangsters and/ Moll, I'd wag/ a twig fag/
   like Bette Davis. Baby Grand/ by Busby Berkley.
1954 He's a student at Union.
   We tumbled out at a cold corner,
   stopped for hot coffee,
   aimed our unpublished canons at each other.
   Tiger & Jack Daw crowd a White Tower.

MARCH 4

A Breathing Heap

1950 How do I know the universe
has no purpose? Science provides
only hypotheses. Intuition may fill me
with conviction. I may believe.
I know nothing.
1951 Life is absurd.
The pointless effort
takes everything.
Body & mind & blood.
What comes back?
1952 Afternoons of a faun.
Wild thing. I fear
the breathing heap that crowds the bonfire.
I dance & sing silence in the wilderness,
leaping among brilliant shadows: *le bon fier.*
1953 Grandstand/ clouds. The rag-/ (stanza)/ time weeds.
Cameras whirred high ci-/ gales in all/ the trees fall-/
ing Technicolor round my/ bedspread Alice Faye.
Byebye,/ Blackbird, call (stanza)/ God at MGM.
Who knew/ I was a-/ live?
1954 Tiger recited me verses.
His sparrows blew, leaves
in the wind, or the leaves
became sparrows & flew.
Then was only the wind.

MARCH 5

I Owe Everything to Other People

1950 Irwin Edman in *Saturday Review*
  & Jean Cocteau in *Flair:* we fear
  the glamour we adore.
  Our movie stars:
  royalty stripped of reality.
1951 Laura confesses herself
  uncertain of my substance:
  "Sometimes I see you flicker.
  You begin to fade.
  I wish you wouldn't."
1952 New confidence blows
  clean into my spirit.
  I was torn by mobs,
  a few friends tend my healing.
  I owe everything to other people.
1953 Well! the/ kids all tried their damnedest
  to/ razz me down. Remote."Boohoo,"/ cried Gilda.
  Theresa, here's something doing,
  irresolution like the cracked,
  anticlimactic rhyme of *a/ the/ Gilda.*
1954 I gave him snatches
  I could remember.
  "I haven't any manuscripts.
  I burned them."
  His laughter ran with white horses.

MARCH 6

Made in USA

1950 Our eyes (red, white & blue)
   roll off assembly lines,
   seeing stars.
   The stars are labeled
   made in USA.
1951 No worry grips me
   more stubborn
   than the always
   unfinished business
   of the poem.
1952 Christopher has fallen.
   His partner runs track. He is discreet.
   He offered Chris a lift home from a meet.
   My friend was still in bed
   on Monday night.
1953 Simplicity is singleness
   in all the parts.
   The poem rules itself
   & cannot bend
   to impertinent conventions.
1954 I expected sunflowers.
   Tiger's room. A sacked altar.
   I sat on heaped brocades in a corner.
   Reformation ruffians played ball
   games in the hall.

MARCH 7

Of Pigs & Pigeons

1950 My father's mother was an Iroquois princess
& the mayor's daughter. How
did he hold office in the nineteenth century? How
did raven beauty come to marry
an illiterate Irish drunk?
1951 "I will never understand you!"
Moma unloads her indignation.
"Darling." (She bristles
when I call her darling.)
"Your lack of understanding is no fault of mine."
1952 To haunt has been my goal.
I can believe the nuance
though I doubt the statement.
I love whatever is indefinite:
moonlight, snowflake, snowfall, shadow, Jack.
1953 Theresa,
I mean to wring free
of all fakery,
sloughing entanglements.
I have broken with Bowwow.
1954 Rude Gert alas!
The splendor in the grass.
O vulgar Holy Ghost.
It takes a pig eons
to become pigeons.

MARCH 8

Telling Mary

1950 Grandmother Raven stroked
my blond head, handled my limbs
like apples to bake in a pie
or peddle to some dumb princess.
"Beauty is the Devil's revenge."
1951 Someone screams
in my ribcage. Bloody cardinal.
I have stayed home from school three days
fitfully reading Carson McCullers.
Neither/nor rattles: *me.*
1952 *The Holy Sinner.*
Epic jingle.
Rhymes & alliterations.
Gargoyles at a gothic
folk dance.
1953 Bluejay chooses to flutter
about my sailing orbit.
Life is not a matter
of lovers. The spirit
shudders, shimmers.
1954 Gertrude
reading on Caedmon:
impervious confidence
like Gabriel telling Mary
the facts of life.

MARCH 9

Beyond This Restlessness

1950 Moma has always preached modesty:
keep your ass covered & don't expect much.
You are only a poor boy.
Her own ambition comes down:
a secret rage. Be best. Take all.
1951 Biography of Diaghilev
in *Atlantic Monthly.*
Were I a dancer I could spin
& leap beyond this restlessness.
Every muscle would ache with fulfillment.
1952 The ad-men can do anything.
Had they imagination with their power
they could promote elegance, whimsy.
The world is their creation.
Why are they so dull about it?
1953 Patience, Theresa,
broods on the wave.
I bring my soul to bed.
We don't have to be cripples.
Love, Jack.
1954 What are little boys made of?
Nothing to be afraid of.
What are little girls made of?
Nothing to be afraid of.
Tigerlily!

MARCH 10

Cage Rage

1950 I walked to school this morning
    & walked on to Joe's.
    He was still sleeping.
    I folded myself
    into his warmth.
1951 I am supposed to be writing
    a novel. I suppose myself to be
    writing a novel. I am not writing
    anything. I am not doing
    anything. Me & the weather.
1952 Laura has never been allowed
    to make a choice or a decision.
    Led by parents
    who are less than she
    & less intelligent than she.
1953 Dixie is directing Noel Coward's
    We Were Dancing. She has cast me
    as the lover. Nerveless
    as an attic demigod
    or lemon twist in somebody's martini.
1954 Riddle: the sky is stalling.
    Riddle: the sky is brawling.
    Riddle: the sky is falling.
    Robin Redbreast is a rage
    that puts all Heaven in a cage.

MARCH 11

Middle March

1950 If I can't attend college
what will I do?
I will go
to New York City.
Do what I can.
1951 *"Il pleure dans mon coeur*
comme it pleut sur la ville."
I laid my books aside. I surrendered
to the dull flood on the raw air.
I wandered all day & evening.
1952 Easy to lead she is impossible to move.
Herself remains untouched.
Her will stands hard & tight,
a terrible rock,
no action in it.
1953 Herr Brain has taken me up.
He intercepts my motions: zany
tangent. The stroke reminds me
of a comic book lightning.
Primary colors on a harmless pulp.
1954 O cherubim. O seraphim.
For whistling girls & crowing hens
hosts in Heaven sigh amens.
For pretty boys & mincing cocks
lots of angels drop their socks.

MARCH 12

What Is This Sudden Exhilaration?

1950 What is it with other people?
   "Where will you be in ten years?"
   What if I were a girl?
   I have stood beside a tree
   & heard the sap run.
1951 No principle of love inspires nature.
   Love does not animate the world.
   I never have been loved.
   I have not loved. I am not loving.
   What is this sudden exhilaration?
1952 After you have taken it
   to pieces you will find it
   isn't there. Look everywhere.
   It isn't there.
   It has escaped you.
1953 He snatches me out of classes,
   catches me at bus stop, coffee shop.
   We drive to other towns
   & other campuses
   to watch movies.
1954 *Desire Under the Elms.*
   Lilian bought me a beer,
   took me to dinner,
   left me at rehearsal.
   Eban took over my body.

MARCH 13

Romancing His Meat

1950 I caution you:
  I'll make the trees grow,
  summon Oberon
  whose antlered brow
  pulls down the stars.
1951 Lust is all.
  I have been its object
  & I have responded.
  The self-conscious mammal
  romances his urgent meat.
1952 A terrible rock.
  That's Laura & Jack.
  In a poem of Lew's
  the rocks are roses.
  Maybe the roses are rocks.
1953 *Limelight, The African Queen,*
  Potemkin, Ten Days That Shook the World,
  Dracula, Night at the Opera.
  Stray acolytes shred
  the decayed cathedral.
1954 It can happen on stage
  that ego drops away:
  a glimpse of universe,
  soundless roar
  behind the mask.

MARCH 14

The Dance

1950 "The wages of sin is death."
The world warns me to beware
the consequences of my doings.
I regret everything I did
not do.
1951 *Le Ballet Russe*
with Danilova, Danielian, Franklin.
Real
dancers on a stage
& me in a magic space.
1952 Bowwow took me to Pearl Primus.
Almost the anniversary of my first ballet.
I am not the same person.
This is not the same world.
THE DANCE.
1953 "Nature, Mr. Allnut, is what we
have been put on earth to rise above," says Rosie.
Like Lew when I was reading *Corydon.*
"Whether it is natural is not the problem.
Is it moral?"
1954 Lew would say Eben
sounds the shallows
of my mother complex.
But Eben in my body is not me
& I am not I in his actions.

MARCH 15

Unruly Mustard

1950 Life without growth?
  Growth without doing?
  Even a vegetable explores
  earth & heaven its own way.
  Unruly mustard!
1951 A clearing in the wilderness
  gathers all eyes
  & tames the savage darkness
  of forgotten lives.
  Sylphides!
1952 Lew's off again.
  Sybil was alone.
  I introduced her to Bowwow.
  We're all a mockery
  demeaning ourselves & the world.
1953 "I never dreamed
  a mere physical experience
  could be so exhilarating!"
  How may we judge life?
  We have still to describe it.
1954 I cross the Union campus.
  I'll stop tomorrow night.
  I'm not a suitor.
  We share a common interest
  in rhyme & reason.

MARCH 16

We Were Dancing

1950 Plato's *Allegory of the Cave.*
  The world is a shadow. Our passions
  waste us on illusions. What passions?
  Perhaps the pagans needed to learn moderation.
  We are dull enough without philosophy.
1951 Lew & Sybil sat behind us.
  Miss Shrimp waved from the balcony.
  Two thousand seats.
  Two thousand pilgrims.
  Quem quaeritis?
1952 Hermes & Theresa
  steered me toward Brooklyn.
  Her room: amethyst rosary,
  Lautrec's *Avril*. A gift:
  Martyre de St Sebastien.
1953 We rehearse our Noel Coward.
  "The gods must have found it
  entrancing–for they smiled."
  Human confusion is play.
  Only divine amusement matters.
1954 Tiger was out.
  A note flapped,
  tacked to the door.
  "Switch on your left.
  Let there be light."

MARCH 17

On the Menu

1950 Hermes & I attended *Winterset*.
  Fate, providence, determinisms.
  I suspect myself a force
  the world & universe & God
  can never tame.
1951 Nina Novak.
  Frederick Franklin
  (misprinted *Granklin* on the menu).
  "What is a grank?"
  sniped Miss Shrimp.
1952 Pens & brushes,
  pastels & oils & inks,
  canvas & wonderful papers
  excite my eyes,
  my nose, my fingertips.
1953 Ross plays the husband.
  His basso wells
  from earth's own womb
  & ravishes all ears.
  But elocution is not acting.
1954 I turned on the light. Took flight.
  Tiger called this morning to complain
  his room crows, haunted,
  a husk, a musk of me
  hovering maverick.

MARCH 18

Hoof & Mouth

1950 I shouldn't creep into a flower.
  I shouldn't trample evening star.
  In real life
  the fabled fittest
  misfits.
1951 "Not grank but grankle," chimed Laura.
  "Rather like a crow."
  The intermissions & applause
  dispel the magic: hoof & mouth
  clamor to exist.
1952 Tanner handed me a letter: *personal.*
  The mystery author requests a meeting.
  I'm to deposit my response
  in Martha Pike,
  Oriental Tale in England.
1953 Lilian, our script girl,
  comes to all rehearsals.
  Our quiet conversations
  counterpoint the screaming
  passes of Dixie & Ross.
1954 Tiger has volunteered
  to hold book
  for *Everyman*
  & *Second Shepherds Play.*
  I bought seats: a pair.

MARCH 19

Yes Is All the World Requires

1950 It is easy to say yes.
   The word is all the world
   requires. I say yes.
   I do no thing.
   No body notices.
1951 Like clouds, like hawks
   they soar.
   I wonder.
   Sweat & pain
   attain impervious spirit.
1952 "On Saturday evening at seven
   you will find me, stranger,
   shivering behind the Pieta
   (a copy) at St Anthony's.
   PS: Be prompt."
1953 Spirit is faster
   than flesh & both
   are lightning
   next to limping
   intellect.
1954 A palindrome
   reads right
   to left & left
   to right.
   I AM: AI!

MARCH 20

Ariel

1950 I'll help myself to a happy ending.
God knows I've hunger enough & reach.
Where's there a table in the wilderness?
Shakespeare. *The Tempest.*
Ariel snatches it away.
1951 What the soul asks of the flesh!
To be realized. To blossom. Everything
for that achievement. Nothing matters
but the purple grove, white arabesques,
the prince invested in black velvet.
1952 Intent on a fable:
Twin Prince.
Sybil has invited
me & Bowwow
to supper.
1953 Whoever I know I am is someone I was last year.
Bluejay babysits for the chairman of sociology.
I kept him company this evening.
Bathing & bedding
the motherless boy.
1954 I'M I.
EWE'R EWE.
WE REW.
Mirror:
mirror.

MARCH 21

Distractions

1950 Joe in profile.
   The arc of his nose
   builds me more
   stately measures:
   Brooklyn Bridge.
1951 Miss Shrimp:
   "I'm just normal I guess."
   The mock apology.
   Fate won't overlook her.
   She'll bitch the monster down.
1952 My twins, in a golden castle in a garden kingdom
   one day, chance upon each other where two halls
   cross. Each, frowning over some irrelevance, takes
   the other's frown to heart. Hearts break & castle
   cracks & kingdom sunders. End of the world.
1953 A springboard day whacked me out
   (with Lilian) of French,
   dodging Professor d'Arc.
   We pranced the snowpatch muddy park,
   surprised by the Friday thaw.
1954 Sunday evenings:
   Television Playhouse.
   Dramas of consequence.
   Actors whose concentration
   erects deep presence.

MARCH 22

Build Upon Nothing

1950 Jack delinquent.
   Joe enacts my truant officer.
   "Couldn't you love a flunky?"
   I wake from a dream of falling.
   His arm is numb.
1951 As we spill into the street
   outside the theater some vulgarian,
   neither sensuous nor witty,
   portends: pretends
   he has himself in hand.
1952 Thyestes recites the fable
   to Sebastian as they stand on a bridge
   over a great river. They go home
   to devour one another & a prince
   is born of their communion.
1953 What I don't know must hurt me.
   I can build nothing upon repression.
   Denial only nurtures illusion.
   Allowance pays the piper.
   Orpheus, look back.
1954 There lies Eben on the page.
   Here stands Eben on the stage.
   Eben will engage
   an audience.
   Legion strikes Heaven.

MARCH 23

A Held Breath

1950 He doesn't see the glory
  in taking each other down
  to mutual perdition.
  Radames, our time
  & oxygen are running out.
1951 I have been reading Shaw's *St Joan.*
  God took her away.
  Men took her apart.
  All that's required
  is ears.
1952 He drove me to a cabin
  by a lake: snow to my knees.
  He stripped me beside a woodstove
  & I shivered
  for his pleasure.
1953 The world is just a lot of facts
  to be accepted & transcended.
  I'm a timebomb ticking
  toward glory. The suspense
  is awful & quotidian.
1954 A character caught
  on the attending breath
  rises like prayer.
  That's why the Puritans
  closed the theaters.

MARCH 24

Vine Leaves

1950 Reason is somehow hateful
in a lover. Joe doesn't know
I'm Jacqueline at school.
If I told him,
it would scare him.
1951 St Joan,
Nijinsky,
drunk Alcibiades
crashing the party
touch me with vine leaves.
1952 The stranger calls himself Walter.
Bowwow, meanwhile, met me at Sybil's.
Lew turned up to tell me
Twin Prince is no story.
It's a "rotten pomegranate."
1953 Some female bitterness
governs Dixie's direction.
"Detach!" she screams.
"You're the Hope Diamond.
What do you care?"
1954 Home all day.
Carried my fever
to rehearsal
riding my clenched
teeth on the cold bus.

MARCH 25

Walking on Hot Water

1950 He tried to reel me
in on common sense.
I teased his flesh
out of the boat.
We staggered on the frolic flood.
1951 Hermes & I watch
Kukla, Fran, and Ollie.
Then we get on the phone
& talk about it.
Lew reads me *Pogo* in the *Star.*
1952 "We must overwhelm
the world with rot!
Only from excrement
springs new life."
I'm eating Proserpine.
1953 I'm to light a cigarette.
I must be diabolic
in the flare of a match.
"The Devil is absolute beauty
& he doesn't give a damn."
1954 Aspirin & cough drops.
Shots of Bourbon on the hour.
The weather buggers Janus.
My fever underscores
lewd omnibus.

MARCH 26

Fetish

1950 He looks me over.
   "You are? Truly? Sixteen! I'm out of my mind!"
   I'm slipping nightly out of Moma's house,
   I'm daily skipping school.
   "Get me a Coke."
1951 Grandmother Raven is dying.
   She has been doing it
   since anybody can remember.
   We have fallen into a habit
   of expecting her miraculous recovery.
1952 Gide's *My Theater:*
   Saul & Bathsheba.
   I must submit myself
   to his mastery
   & learn restraint.
1953 Dixie let no one touch me.
   She did my make up:
   perfection by Snow Queen.
   I felt like a fetish.
   The other actors grow resentful.
1954 Missed the last bus
   & lugged my hot brain downtown.
   Found a stranger
   to take me home. Dawn.
   Delirium can't make it.

MARCH 27

Outside the Garden

1950 In a timeless garden
   the spirit dwells & cares
   nothing for fear & the law.
   It does not even care
   to mock the world.
1951 Grandmother Raven
   stirred the porridge
   of my childbrain
   with a shaman finger
   cackling, "Goldenrod."
1952 "Walter, Walter, lead me to the altar."
   He poses me under spots
   & watches behind a big camera
   while I hand myself over:
   Flash Gordon!
1953 I struck the match.
   Briefly I felt like stone.
   Then an utter relaxation flooded me.
   "It was the most sexual moment
   in all history."
1954 Lilian & Henry J collected me.
   We went to see *The Second Shepherd's Play*.
   The Middle English meter tuned my trembling.
   "I was flaid with a sweven."
   Tiger joined us over beer & sausages.

MARCH 28

He Turns Out All the Lights

1950 The future swings
   whip or worm. Crackerjack
   seeks the prize
   still wrapped in wax,
   the dark & narrow box.
1951 "Your mother," she would allow,
   "is a pretty woman & your dad,
   like his father small, is handsome.
   You, child! You & I are Beauty."
   Then she'd cough up blood.
1952 He turns out all the lights.
   I hear his bare feet whisper on the floor.
   Something like flesh falls across my back
   & something like a mad fish gasps,
   chokes on searing velvet.
1953 Ross got drunk
   & dropped his pants.
   "Yes," mocked Dixie.
   "I can see it's a cock.
   But what's special about it?"
1954 I puked out all
   the foul & silly
   years I've lived & died.
   Woke to the smell of onions.
   Moma made soup.

MARCH 29

A Few Brown Teeth

1950 Happily
ever after
abandon hope
all you
who enter here.
1951 She would cower in shawls beside a fire
on a summer afternoon & I'd consider her few
brown teeth & ticking face & wonderful
wild hair. Old woman
like the coaldust on the windowsill.
1952 I promised to see Walter Wednesday.
Bowwow, meanwhile, escorts me
to bars & movies:
Death of a Salesman,
Sister Carrie.
1953 I thought it rather fine,
much the best part of him indeed.
Lilian caught my eye pertly.
So I blushed
& said nothing.
1954 Beautiful soup
wafts: my salvation.
Lilian called
to roast my Tiger.
I'd have eaten him raw.

MARCH 30

Modern American Poetry

1950 From Keith in Providence to Kettle
who was reading *Death in the Afternoon.*
The soul-surrendering epistle
served to mark a page & be forgotten.
Kettle, you are a careless confidant.
1951 Dad & Aunt Nod
talk my old savage round to Rome.
She was the only Episcopalian
in the family since the last
of her three healthy sisters died.
1952 I danced down State Street singing:
Bowwow's my gentleman,
Bowwow's my gentleman,
Bowwow's my gentleman,
I'm his gutter girl.
1953 Modern American Poetry.
Either Emily
hymns acid
or Walt Whitman
yawps.
1954 I steep
in sweet recovery.
A letter comes from Hermes:
cock's crow over his virginity
scattered like corn to the chickens.

MARCH 31

Letters from Providence

1950 This Keith in Providence goes west.
His father has cursed him out. He doesn't
want a desk job or a college education. He loves
no one & has no hope of loving anyone. He'll hitch
to Oregon & level forests & read books.
1951 Rainfall: I am
the flood,
the spill,
the flow,
the miracle.
1952 Lew broods.
Yellow-green life buds
in the cemetery. Crooked
back streets bode. I showed Sybil
where Joe used to live.
1953 Spirit lurks. The power
beyond the image
by which we call
the image up
or cry it down.
1954 Now loom Hermes & Miriam.
He talked about her at Thanksgiving.
She was one of Mr. Bear's party at Christmas.
She's from Sweden out of Poland.
I remember her accent.

APRIL 1

Wouldn't It Be Dumb?

1950 Wouldn't it be dumb to fall in love
with the immaterial
author of a letter
abandoned, then abducted
from a library book?
1951 Her small head nested in grey fur.
Her eyes peeped out. The red mouth gaped.
"Come, John, help me find these titles."
The words found him
like fleas.
1952 Hot fudge, friend
of Hermes & Theresa,
before she left home for college
seduced her brother.
She has sent me a box.
1953 The entombment for reflection.
The entombment for selection.
The entombment to make ready.
The entombment. The increase.
The root. The star.
1954 She wore a black sweater
& navy skirt over black tights.
Lilian declared it "an awkward mix."
Mr. Bear played Eartha Kitt over & over.
I danced with everyone singing *Lilac Wine*.

APRIL 2

Candyland

1950 I believe in Keith
sheathed in a Hemingway casket.
Sounds shape words.
Words shape identity.
Spirit attaches matter.
1951 Moma spoke of girls
who loved men
who loved money.
Pimps.
What must it be like to be sold?
1952 The box contains
one shell of a horseshoe crab,
her naked back on canvas,
sketches of cats,
feathered mountings of old flies.
1953 Hart Crane, from Candyland,
jumped into the sea.
His mother had her ashes
scattered from BB.
Woman, like nature, cannot be defeated.
1954 When Hitler invaded Poland,
Miriam was five or six
hiding with a younger brother
in the house of her Polish nurse.
"But the Poles could not be trusted."

APRIL 3

Seeds

1950 *Morals* is my title.
Jamie is my hero.
No father.
An uncle: buffoon,
unreachable drunk.
1951 Among the seeds that caution cannot sort
do secret sympathies perceive what's what?
What opened me to Sybil
so she would bring
me Baudelaire & Lew?
1952 She menstruates twice yearly
if all goes well."Except
a corn of wheat
fall into the ground and die,
it abideth alone."
1953 Living is
a dirty work
that mines
a diamond:
THE WORDS.
1954 Two children
fleeing an army,
a nation, a world
crushing itself out
against the Jews.

APRIL 4

A Pile of Stones

1950 His mother knows only
  a boy should comb his hair
  & brush his teeth.
  Her whole catechism
  breakfasts & buttons up.
1951 I didn't know
  such poetry would strip
  me to the bone.
  Always be quick
  & risk it.
1952 Dear Fudge,
  the will (or won't)
  looks childish
  to fascist shopkeepers.
  I love your box.
1953 Bluejay flickers in a tree.
  He's quicker than the eye.
  For every bird
  there's a bush
  & a pile of stones.
1954 Hermes showed me sketches
  Miriam made of hungry faces
  & voluptuous flowers.
  How shall I shape
  to Hermes & Miriam?

APRIL 5

Dry Chalk on Slate

1950 Schoolmates
face homeplates
or goalposts.
Sport is all the talk,
dry chalk on slate.
1951 Perversity
is a dove
that broods
on the suspended wave.
Let there be floods.
1952 I disapprove
of discipline
except the crafting
of a poem.
I hunger for trouble.
1953 John Wayne
rams his big rod
into a camera.
Worlds are made.
Bodies blossom.
1954 Doors can be opened.
Lilian hears a tick.
I listen for the tock.
Hell demands a reason.
BOOM.

APRIL 6

Hard White Droppings

1950 Jamie airs
  his attic room
  with radio.
  Woolworth & movies
  tease his need.
1951 Laura must touch me.
  I kissed her
  & we fell
  to a useless heat,
  frantic & unfriendly.
1952 I will not cultivate disinterest.
  Divinity achieves its will
  through our attention & involvement.
  Curious leaf, inquisitive raindrop,
  terrifying eye increase me.
1953 I have asked questions.
  I have hung around the halls.
  Bluejay attends no classes.
  He has moved out of the dorm.
  His hard white droppings baffle.
1954 Like St Augustine
  I heard a child singing
  a catch off the wind:
  "I am a chicken
  on the mountain."

APRIL 7

Alienations

1950 An ignorant stranger
   teaches him joy & woe.
   End of the story.
   He's mute & alone.
   Straight morals estrange.
1951 Naturalism
   endlessly induces,
   slicing at life:
   data is data.
   Stars seem vastly distant & indifferent.
1952 Hitler
   & Stalin
   & Mad Ave
   interpret
   the same Mammon.
1953 The church
   keeps God
   in gilded cages.
   Fundamentalism
   is idolatry.
1954 Tiger takes a cold to bed.
   I sit at his feet & we talk
   about people in books.
   We would rather our lives
   were poems than a novel.

APRIL 8

Saint Augustine in Carthage

1950 *Toxophily:*
   love of archery.
   How skills embrace the kill!
   Saint Augustine
   in Carthage.
1951 Stars seem vastly distant & indifferent.
   They burn inside us.
   Though ego aches & rages,
   no indifference approaches the indifference
   my soul holds toward the world.
1952 Bowwow's greenwood gang delight.
   His pathos saps.
   Walter fascinates:
   freakish & solitary.
   What is love?
1953 How do I judge
   the church?
   What do I know
   of the spirit?
   Nothing moves me.
1954 He wore his coat under the covers.
   Grey fur purred at his ears,
   his face all flush & fever.
   I felt the room fill up
   with little animals.

APRIL 9

Little Animals

1950 A girl called Laura,
the other freak at school,
has been wafting
toward me on the wind
of shared abuse.
1951 Character develops like a rose,
like the planets blowing on the sunstem,
like the history of earth
or a dog
making his bed.
1952 Two lovers keep me busy.
Their jealousy improves my cunning.
I brag about my promiscuity
to Laura & Hot Fudge.
Jack Daw can learn to mock the human voice.
1953 Ethos, says Aristotle, is directed energy:
to do, to make, to know.
I am ignorant,
a do no dodo,
makeless as a maid.
1954 My head, my heart, my lungs,
monk cells
of my brain & body
swarm with little animals.
Wild life!

APRIL 10

A Spilled Sack

1950 Hermes listens
   & befriends.
   He witnesses my daily
   humiliation & stands by.
   I tell him all my secrets.
1951 "Sally go round the sun,
   Sally go round the moon,
   Sally go round the chimneypots
   on a Saturday afternoon."
   Wind & the worm whirl & adorn the dancer.
1952 His yellow Studebaker idles in the rain.
   "Bowwow, why are you sad?
   Are you angry? Because
   I ate four petals off
   the rose you gave me?"
1953 Lunch in the lurching cafeteria.
   The crowd shakes out a bluejay:
   new job,
   new apartment,
   old song.
1954 A grey squirrel
   heads down
   the hollow trunk
   to the root
   & the nut sack.

APRIL 11

What Are Little Boys Made Of?

1950 Forsythia springs from my fingers,
showers me with petals & raindrops.
I glisten & want to strip
among the whipping branches
in a gray rain.
1951 The judgment of the state
arrived today that I am not
college material. They hope
I will find a rut
to which I am better suited.
1952 We sit forever in the purring convertible.
Raindrops pobble the canvas. Wipers whip.
His melancholy overwhelms me
& I take the reins & wrap
my tongue around his leaping heart.
1953 Roman dormers look
to gothic St Mary's.
He served me cake & wine.
We shared a cigarette.
Me & my big mouth.
1954 What are little boys made of?
Nothing to be afraid of.
A music ravages the mountain.
When is advent?
Where is the Pied Piper?

APRIL 12

Fol de Rol

1950 I come to Joe
   drenched to the skin
   at his bedside, my arms
   full of flower swaths,
   switches of yellow forsythia.
1951 "Gentlemen: I am not stupid.
   I have been oversexed
   & indolent." Jack Sprat
   will eat
   no fat.
1952 Bowwow,
   it's hard
   to know
   who's who
   in our little fairy tale.
1953 I offer him experience & wit.
   He wants a little rose buddy,
   a little fool.
   The hackneyed heads
   still *fol de rol.*
1954 The crew despise the actors.
   Actors hate the crew
   & one another.
   The director is a tyrant imbecile.
   Always the same show down.

APRIL 13

A Bright Blankness

1950 Nijinsky stood on air
a moment & withdrew.
The rest is silence.
He was the alien
art could not detain.
1951 Fate meant me
to be murdered
by the candyman,
the goon in the green sedan.
I was too dumb to die.
1952 The Texans,
hosts of golden daffodils,
continue the entertainment.
Cynic Mash, Rex Buddha
ease my waywardness.
1953 I left him
& spitting
feathers
tramped
the town.
1954 Eban casts me out.
I move in a bright
blankness
knowing nothing.
I am not.

APRIL 14

Dragonflies

1950 Nijinsky:
unfathomable merman.
Nijinsky:
profound fabula.
Nijinsky.
1951 Laura takes me bugging
by Saint Panther's pond.
We're friends again.
I couldn't hold a candle
to a dragonfly.
1952 Bowwow has passed out
in the shower. The party
writhes & riddles.
Mash says, "Hubba hubba."
Buddha says, "Reeling! Reeling!"
1953 Took a sixty-minute shower at the gym.
Talked Lilian out of French.
We found a little coffee shop on Lark.
Later I fell asleep: my head
in her lap in the park.
1954 Eben:
an intimate
alien pain.
The perfect illumination
of simply *other*.

APRIL 15

Bright Carp

1950 Laura stumbled upon me in the stacks.
   She sprawled on the floor,
   hugging some books
   to clean knees,
   & chattered at me.
1951 She wore her newsboy knickers & fat cap.
   The sun was a slow barge like her sensible shoes
   sucking through mud & sky.
   I tripped like Lady Slipper in the wake.
   The haunted pond hangs with bright carp.
1952 Mortimer built a fire in an ashtray.
   I knelt to the flame & roasted & ate
   rose petals thinking of Proserpine
   & pomegranate seeds & how we laughed
   when the old earth opened & said *arf!*
1953 Lilian showed up this morning at The Bull.
   I was meditating on a mug of coffee.
   We missed our classes while I told
   sad tales of Bluejay & Bowwow.
   Finally, Laura.
1954 Dame Agnes explained,
   "These are the symptoms of a total concentration."
   Symptoms. Art is pathology. She also said,
   "Your absorption in the arts, child, brings me back.
   Such devotion was a symptom of my generation."

APRIL 16

O Wheel

1950 She spoke mostly cabbages
   & kings & things & books:
   Arthurian stuff,
   animal tales.
   I recommended *Other Voices, Other Rooms.*
1951 I admired
   the precision
   of her little murders.
   Who'd guess those pudgy paws
   could be so nice?
1952 Walter has moved to the lake.
   I wait for the bus.
   Rod's Records pumps out Kaye & Ray.
   O Wheel of Fortune.
   You'll Feel Better if You Cry.
1953 Letters come from Laura
   & go unanswered.
   She gasps
   in the shallows
   of my psyche.
1954 A last performance & cast party.
   Seeing friends off on a very late train.
   Lilian will drive home in the morning.
   I lay me down to haunted sleep
   & wake to spring vacation.

APRIL 17

Shadows

1950 On Uncle Skunk's bike
  I pedaled out to meet
  Laura's family: Toad Hall.
  Where do we come from?
  Changelings.
1951 We played a game of toss.
  The sun was our ball.
  "Clap hands, clap hands,
  hie Jack Dandy."
  How well she knows her rhymes!
1952 He meets my bus in Saratoga,
  drives me through the ghost town,
  a hand in my pants.
  He likes to ring changes on old saws.
  "A stitch in time gathers no moss."
1953 I had a little shadow.
  He went in & out with me.
  What use?
  What use
  was more than I could see.
1954 Jesus is condemned to death.
  He takes the cross. He falls the first time.
  He meets his blessed mother. Simon helps him.
  Veronica wipes his face.
  He falls the second time.

APRIL 18

The Winged Foot

1950 "I know
  all about sex
  & babies.
  Clearly they found me
  under a cabbage."
1951 What will I do?
  A serpent sea
  rises against me.
  I will swallow mad Atlantic
  & spew havoc from my ears.
1952 I am the bird in hand,
  the devil's playground.
  "If this my mother knew
  her heart would break in two,"
  utters the goose girl.
1953 Lilian wants to know
  more about Hermes.
  "That's a whole 'nother story."
  My friend. My friend.
  The winged foot.
1954 He speaks to the women of Jerusalem.
  He falls the third time. He is stripped.
  He is nailed to the cross.
  He dies on the cross.
  He is laid in the tomb.

APRIL 19

Awful Shadows

1950 We cycled out.
   The countryside met us on shared breezes.
   All seemed one spunky toss & tumble:
   spinning hills
   & knees.
1951 Bittersweet is best.
   The awful windows
   of St John's
   at sunset
   burning.
1952 Warm Walter brings a basin
   of warm water,
   soap & towels.
   Straight razor.
   Shaves my genitals.
1953 We have roped
   the high mountains.
   We have outrun the sky.
   The gods have had to move
   inside.
1954 Hermes is here
   & gone. We celebrated
   the good news of Miriam.
   Easter weekend.
   Resurrection!

APRIL 20

Fattening Hansel

1950 She spoke of her parents.
"My daddy harps
the world's praise
on his golf bag."
Hole in one.
1951 Walked home from Sybil's
devouring a still warm loaf
of Lew's baking.
Riddles & wine
while the dough rose.
1952 The lights go out,
candles at my head & feet,
& he undresses in the dark.
Psyche must not look.
Sisters, what do you advise?
1953 A raunchy old ranch hand
roped me off the bus stand
& I never got to school.
We rode his hotel bed all day
drinking beer from brown bottles.
1954 Tiger has come again.
He calls me from downtown.
His empty dorm roars like a conch.
We fill his room with tulips.
The red ones crow. "Stop thief!"

APRIL 21

Tripping the Moon

1950 My dad says
you're a damned fairy.
Are you a damned fairy?
What is a fairy?
Oh.
1951 Repose in these sweet sorrows then.
Something moves in lilac shadow.
Wine & bread await.
The sky booms Dr. Jekyll.
The sky looms Mr. Hyde.
1952 The claptrap bus
drowns out my singing
the long way home.
"A trip to the moon
on gossamer wings."
1953 Sneaky feet lisp & whisper.
I snack on raindrops,
seeking meat.
A matinee!
O April, weep for me.
1954 Red & yellow tulips:
cocks & crowns.
On clumsy old platters,
crocks & clowns,
Four Saints in Three Acts.

APRIL 22

Nobody Barks Back

1950 We rival Mab & Oberon.
  She climbs a tree & shoots me
  aping archer from above.
  Now we are playmates
  & such stuff.
1951 The seventh-grade teachers
  sent Laura to an analyst.
  She barked at them.
  She barked at him.
  "Nobody barked back."
1952 Laura faints a lot.
  Bowwow's distempered.
  My cat had kittens.
  Hermes & Theresa write.
  Hot Fudge invites *post scriptum.*
1953 Truant again: I take
  my stand at an urinal.
  Grim & eternal white of it.
  Pink, disinfectant wafer.
  Jack of all trade.
1954 Brando's Mark Antony,
  Garbo's Ninotchka, Camille,
  & Garland's Dorothy in Oz.
  Above the chimney tops
  you'll find me.

APRIL 23

Death by Water

1950 A stranger spirit
  possesses my puppet limbs.
  I walk the common world.
  Invisible gold enfolds my clay.
  Inviolate enigma moves me.
1951 Denver takes up Listerine.
  She is too good for him.
  He's no different from the rest.
  A girl is just a rag,
  a rubber to brag about.
1952 Our Sunday afternoons
  repeat a pattern.
  Sybil's adorations slide
  toward self-contempt.
  Then Lew explodes.
1953 Cocksucker!
  This odd bird
  that feeds on flies
  feeds as it falls upon the drafts of chance.
  I shall die by drowning in the Gentlemen's.
1954 We brought apples to his room
  & ate them standing at the window.
  The empty campus made the moonlight.
  The chapel's strokes, for midnight,
  swept us away on the tidings.

APRIL 24

Dragging Enchantment

1950 I drag enchantment
   through the streets
   & wear it always.
   Joe cannot strip me,
   doesn't know.
1951 Laura fed shrimps
   to the four of us
   after the movies.
   Denver & Listerine fell
   to "heavy necking."
1952 Wine or gin is catalyst.
   I am the essential witness.
   All her worship will not win him.
   The more he is made an idol,
   the more he must behave badly, like the gods.
1953 The fall is accomplished.
   Having drunk myself down
   on Moma's Christmas Bourbon,
   I wake in my own bed.
   Nothing will do.
1954 Jack Tiger
   like a gleaming flood
   fell on the lawn & saw stars.
   I'll brook no testacies
   against our interlucence.

APRIL 25

Cracker

1950 Do not think that you can touch me.
 I do not think I can outreach
 the flood that weaves around me.
 Ora pro nobis.
 Ora pro nobis, Mare.
1951 We might have sat apart
 appraising their skill
 unlikely as *twa corbies*
 awaiting the kill.
 "Where shall we gang and din?"
1952 Their battles are acts of congress.
 He slams out the door.
 She sinks, all tears & trembling, into a chair.
 I am the village midwife, ancient & surprised,
 clucking beside her ear like mourning doves.
1953 Grandmother Raven's Cracker,
 a thieving crow, got caught
 & cast into a privy.
 He rose again.
 Grandmother preferred him to a phoenix.
1954 In purple patches
 we have still
 one wit between us:
 testacies
 is good.

APRIL 26

Ludus Chiaroscuro

1950 A poem appropriates eternity.
 Like a scythe, it harvests me.
 Like worms, explores.
 Like rainfall,
 endows me grace.
1951 I kissed her opened mouth,
 charging the dragon in its moaning cavern;
 handled her breasts & lay my ear between them.
 I could hear the princess beating to be freed.
 My little seal stood barking on the rocks.
1952 I feel endangered.
 I am baffled.
 I love them both.
 I do not understand why
 love is no help.
1953 I study Untermeyer in the old edition
 Lew gave me with his sappy marginalia,
 poets' pictures clipped from the *Times,*
 & four red arrows pointing at Elinor Wylie's
 "Live like the velvet mole."
1954 *Interlucation,*
 interlucent,
 interlude.
 Ludus chiaroscuro
 in a sacred wood.

APRIL 27

Gods & Caesars

1950 I'm failing everything. Burden spoke to me
representing "a concerned faculty." My truancy
has been reported home. Moma wants to know
where I've been spending my days.
It's time to render unto Caesar.
1951 She seemed a sweet bird singing in my hands.
How dear! How fierce!
How clumsily she groped Excaliber.
O sword! O stones! Girl,
leave me a piece of that.
1952 Walked home from the station,
from Sunday in Manhattan with my friends.
Moma surprised me sitting up with Dad
& a pot of coffee at the kitchen table.
Grandmother Raven has died.
1953 I am the spring breeze.
I am the first day of the week.
Ross is directing Williams'
death of D H Lawrence
& wants Lilian for Frieda.
1954 Lilian led me to the park
so we could be alone.
We can get married in September.
Her parents will support us.
Do I think we should?

APRIL 28

The Farce of the World

1950 When you're 16,
there's no way to turn
from the farce of the world
that slams you head over hell's
dull rut.
1951 Today I cannot tolerate
her warm hand on my arm.
"Go sharpen your claws
on the woodwork."
Pussy willow.
1952 She'd do it unexpected in the end.
Her sly & solitary going means
she'll occupy heaven
like a pearl in its oyster:
eternity's prize ulcer.
1953 I wrote to Laura I'd come
to her Freshman Class Weekend
& act her beau at yet another ball,
Pease to her Mustardseed
at one more picnic.
1954 Hermes & Miriam meet us
as we stumble out of British Lit.
Hot Fudge looms behind them.
She drove the couple to Connecticut:
they married. Miriam is pregnant.

APRIL 29

Born to be Hanged

1950 Childhood is over.
Empty slogans
blunt the air.
Every little piggy
goes to market.
1951 I'm reading *Tom Jones*.
Sometimes a book
speaks an embrace
from my very own heart:
BORN TO BE HANGED.
1952 My uncles hanked my Grampa Bean
out of a dive & dragged him to the baths.
"Shave and a haircut: two bits."
In a borrowed suit,
he's two shakes & a lamb's tail.
1953 Edward Arlington Robinson
taunts the American dream:
mindless echoes whimpering
failure, failure, failure,
failure, failure.
1954 Nasty Jack, with Jilian,
plans an autumn wedding.
Hermes, of good repute,
mops his spilt milk
before the piper.

APRIL 30

Among the Elders

1950 Joe made us lunch
  & we sat down
  to plan our future.
  How Murphy has fattened
  on our minstrelsy!
1951 "You haven't done ten minutes'
  work all afternoon." Thus
  Tanner popped the blade
  from some old wound
  & the sob rose with it.
1952 With the pint in her purse & a teaspoon
  Aunt Nod administers a Bourbon dosage,
  keeping the old man on his feet.
  He's all his children know of shame & glamour.
  He's enough.
1953 Sandburg flatters
  like a devil who, dulled
  on ages of success & ownership,
  beats a Salvation Army drum:
  The People Yes.
1954 Hermes complains the elders
  have been wailing
  wrath & woe long distance
  since Monday night. "Suddenly
  they're Jewish."

MAY 1

Truant Airs

1950 We'll dwell in Syracuse.
   I will attend university.
   Joe will spin
   blue rooms
   on the truant air.
1951 I trod home weeping.
   I wept in my bed.
   I wonder a body
   holds so much
   water & salt.
1952 Grandmother Raven's body
   waits for burial. Daddy & Aunt Nod
   have dressed her in lavender
   & all the hoarded diamonds of better days.
   Orchids everywhere.
1953 Walt Whitman
   beats railroad & lilac
   back to Adam
   with a workman's
   hard contempt for facts.
1954 Miriam vomits a lot.
   What of her education?
   Her career?
   Ancient shames
   claim shabby sacrifices.

MAY 2

The Radiant Bride

1950 Everywhere I turn is me.
   Everyone I meet is me.
   Passing moment. Passing stranger.
   Stone & star & butt & bee.
   Gnat & nut & knot & tree.
1951 I don't know why I wept.
   I know there was no stopping
   & my theme was what
   have I ever done well?
   I have never done anything well.
1952 Diamonds & orchids were her rage.
   Meanwhile her face reposes.
   I discover she is beautiful.
   Bones like a cathedral. Hair
   like perfect night, enigmatic underworld.
1953 Her mind is
   an enchanting,
   an enchanted
   thing she sings toward being
   Marianne Moore.
1954 I fear for Hermes,
   want Miriam to make him happy,
   want to occupy her like a dybbuk,
   seize & shake her to bliss,
   make her his radiant bride.

MAY 3

Altars

1950 The stranger in the mirror,
the boy in the pool, I see.
But seeing through can't fathom.
He is the other.
Me/not/me.
1951 Sleep fell hot & heavy as volcano flow.
Moma burned
lights all night,
cracked my door once,
said nothing.
1952 Odd moments of childhood
stir my memory.
The family felt closer then.
The cosmos is expanding.
Cousins & uncles wink in the velvet & recede.
1953 I open like a hungry flower reading Eliot,
swooning to the music & the misery.
Limbo & Gotterdamerung.
That weary hermaphrodite,
our long lost soul.
1954 She weeps at me as if I understand.
She doesn't feel my awe.
We are the first fruit & the lamb
slain on the altar of new life.
She'll bear the first babe of our generation.

MAY 4

Will Living Teach Me Who I Am?

1950 Will living teach me who I am?
   Laura meets me afternoons at County P.
   We stroll homeward under trees.
   She asks me embarrassing questions.
   I tell her no lies.
1951 On Saturday I strode downtown
   behind dark glasses in a world of haze & halo.
   Bought *The Counterfeiters & Journal* in a volume.
   Sought comfort with Hermes & Sybil & Laura.
   I can read & I have friends.
1952 Returning from the cemetery, Moma
   spoke the unexpected epitaph: "She was
   my friend." The raven showed only my Moma
   the far side of her heart where graceful
   serpents sunned among apples & bees.
1953 He & his better maker
   lost their souls to anti-semitism.
   Ezra thinks the Jews made banks.
   Christendom made banks to be the prison of the Jews.
   The Jews made God. Their God made freedom from Man's will.
1954 I wanted them to meet my Tiger.
   He arrived with a tiny gift.
   A velvet rabbit in a nest
   of real fur brooding on amber.
   "Dumb bunnies make your dreams come true."

MAY 5

Hanging on the Winged Heel

1950 We sit on the cobble bridge.
  She chases a city mouse across the road.
  Gay breezes catch my breath.
  "Blowing is only an expression."
  We talk about my sex life & the prom.
1951 Lew kissed me.
  Sybil had withdrawn into the *Times*.
  We had the floor & Bruegels.
  Stench of frolic peasants.
  "Odor of human bodies is holy."
1952 They had in common Grampa Bean the terrible
  husband, terrifying in-law; also my Dad,
  the child groom of their womanly contempt.
  They shared an escapist passion for the ten-cent
  talkies' tick & flicker.
1953 The true inheritor
  of Whitman-Emily's
  androgenous America,
  Hart Crane
  crosses Brooklyn Bridge.
1954 They drove away yesterday,
  Hot Fudge at the wheel.
  What does Hermes feel?
  He has been very quiet
  hanging on the winged heel.

MAY 6

Touched to Consciousness

1950 Facts, fancies, faces consort.
   Pain & the commonplace,
   monster & midden
   burnish Westminster,
   mass like millepore.
1951 I closed my eyes
   & saw into the candles.
   Beacon worlds of bliss & woe
   where brilliant creatures
   fall & dream & do.
1952 I was brought to Dietrich in a bunting.
   My diaper turned to gold in the massed darkness
   while my women wept & thrilled toward Lombard,
   Colbert, Shearer. Gable, Tracy. Mickey Rooney's
   Puck touched me to consciousness in 1936.
1953 Herr Brain
   teased me out of the library,
   bought me a beer & accused,
   "You never seem to think
   about tomorrow."
1954 When I told Tiger, "Lilian
   & I will marry in September,"
   he clapped me to him.
   "Congratulations!" So,
   le roi s'amuse.

MAY 7

Hungry Heart

1950 My dad
chased me across the kitchen
& knocked me into a closet
because I called him
tedious & crude.
1951 Flames rise. Tears fall.
"Sybil, I'm sorry."
She smiles at my apology.
My jaded brain remembers
how she brought me to him as an offering.
1952 Meanwhile I peep in on sucking kittens.
Twinkle, twinkle, little star.
"Moma," I venture,
"How did you meet
my dad?"
1953 Herr Brain
judges me giddy.
His idea of smart
is pessimism
in the manner of our moping century.
1954 "Let me fill again my hungry heart.
Blind me with your charms
and all the stardust in the sky.
Take me in your arms
and then goodbye."

MAY 8

Piping Peter

1950 Pick. Pick.
Hey, Peter Piper,
where is the pied
world of the living?
Where is Puck?
1951 Time weeps.
I see it in my eyes,
this less than silence,
less than darkness:
light years.
1952 "These Polish girls are bold.
She was coming off work
out of Woolworths.
I was waiting for the light.
'Hi, Handsome!' says she."
1953 Why should I pride myself on feeling woe
as anyone can do?
Henceforth allow:
even a foolish delight
distinguishes the fool.
1954 Old song. My heart
is an old song bag,
the Tin Pan alien.
"Moonlight becomes you."
There's a metamorphosis.

MAY 9

The Other Way Round

1950 Prince Lard
  presides.
  Disenchanted.
  Burden says,
  "Swim with the current."
1951 Where will I be in *Ten-Years-Ten*?
  Lew has deserted us, gone to seed
  his brother's farm in Ballstone.
  Sybil comforts me with ice cream.
  I bring the beer.
1952 "I never!
  It was just the other way."
  The other way round as the world is.
  She was seventeen. "Hi, Beautiful!"
  He had a wife & son somewhere.
1953 We stopped at Carp's for a fish fry.
  Everyone was there & pretty high.
  Herr Brain & Dixie argued about homosexuality.
  He thinks it is a rose by any other name.
  She feels it is a crying shame.
1954 Laura becomes Lilian.
  Bowwow, Bluejay, Mr Bear
  become Tiger.
  We become moonlight
  or dark of the moon.

MAY 10

Popular Music

1950 "Laura, the fact
   is you're dying
   to go to the prom
   & I can't
   understand it."
1951 Beer really comes in your mouth.
   Whiskey swells & smarts the throat.
   Alcohol is the world's way
   to sublimate the universal
   blowboy.
1952 "I found a million-dollar baby
   at the five-and-ten-cent store."
   He was the bad boy & speakeasy bootlegger.
   She was a good girl & pretty.
   Prohibition was about to be amended.
1953 Herr Brain thinks homosexuality
   is an immunity, an artist's
   reservation of his necessary
   irresponsibility.
   He don't know many queers.
1954 Pussycat, Pussycat,
   where have you been?
   He's been to Manhattan
   to look at the queens.
   My smile is an umbrella.

MAY 11

At Lovers' Heels

1950 "I'm not hot to go
but I want to be taken."
Two for the show?
"The droll show."
Troll, I won't say no.
1951 Of course I wrote
a very bad story
about the three of us,
turning good bread
to stones.
1952 They didn't stand a chance. I was a tickle
determined to be born. Prohibition & a Great
Depression couldn't stop me. I sped his wildness
to her shame & left them nothing. I have heard
the bedsprings sing their anger & my name.
1953 Dixie sang a hymn to procreation:
sex is the divine in man; our seed
is our eternal. She doesn't give a damn
when Simple Simon simpers over Sadsack Sam.
"But I weep to see genius wasted."
1954 Jealousy is
a dull inheritance
I learned
at lovers'
heels.

MAY 12

Dumb Rages

1950 Not speaking to Dad.
 He is not speaking to me.
 His cigarette smoke
 woos the room.
 The sexy man exhales.
1951 I should report us racy
 as Fielding reports his Tom.
 I must slough
 this sequin skin.
 How darkly the diamondback rattles.
1952 I have lain in bed & listened
 to their intercourse. I whipped them on.
 Master Jack,
 at the root
 of the mystery.
1953 Let Dixie & Herr Brain conduct
 their ignorant debate
 until Doomsday.
 Homosexuality
 is not one thing.
1954 Tiger took off for Manhattan
 & tramped. I sat with the lamps
 in his empty room & waited.
 Sunday. Midnight. He sails in
 to my dumb rage.

MAY 13

Chink, Chank, Chunk

1950 Moma may nag
  & Dad may shun.
  They never dare
  honestly to know
  me. Me. Me.
1951 Death laughs at hand.
  I felt him yapping at my heels
  as I ran from the house downtown
  & across the stone bridge.
  Tugboat & barge.
1952 Grandmother Raven is dead. She has taken
  a little boy to be her guide & company.
  The child I was, the child she shaped with stories
  of vengeful life & vengeful women
  while she shivered & I shed July.
1953 Dear Dixie,
  heterosexuals
  all look alike
  to me as chinks
  or chanks or chunks.
1954 I had hoped to hear from Hermes.
  Comes a chatter.
  They were married again
  in synagogue to please her parents.
  They have found an apartment.

MAY 14

Jack, Robin's On

1950 Miss Shrimp calls Laura
  childish & just right
  for Jack Candle.
  "Quick, Laura,
  what's the feminine for *prick*?
1951 Gide perceives
  unlearning is the way
  back to the spirit.
  Dumb kiss in the dark
  stirs Beauty.
1952 Hermes'Theresa
  gave me a scallop
  of scent
  called *Shalimar*.
  I'll waft on this wave.
1953 Fairyland
  is another
  nation.
  Each faun
  has his face.
1954 Miriam's
  morning glories
  have gone by.
  Weave, weave,
  the singing nest.

MAY 15

Hermes Only Wonders

1950 *"Princess* of course."
  Exit Miss Shrimp.
  Hermes only wonders:
  "Why you're so thick
  with that girl."
1951 In sudden heat
  I went to a barber
  & had myself
  terribly shorn
  for the stake.
1952 Bowwow, however,
  bought me lush bottles
  of *Aphrodisia* & *Tigress*,
  animal fruits,
  jewels of Faberge.
1953 *Spectre of the Rose.*
  Morality imposes,
  but spirit eludes:
  unfathomable seahorse,
  infinite hummingbird.
1954 "Most subject is the fattest soil to weeds."
  I am preparing to direct
  scenes from Shakespeare's
  Henry Four Part Two.
  Prodigal Hal inherits.

MAY 16

I Prance in the Streets

1950 I dare not suppose he's jealous.
  Everyone erects such cynical defenses.
  Every thing, meanwhile, is beautiful!
  I prance in the streets
  & talk to myself.
1951 Dick, a new boy
  come to page at County P,
  buzzes in on me
  & Sybil & Laura & me.
  His father makes wine.
1952 Walter has been a Roxy
  chorus boy. We watch "Your Hit Parade"
  on his little TV.
  He gossips
  about the dancers.
1953 "Wheat from the chaff,
  sheep from the goats," they say.
  I turn the other
  hot, cross bun
  & hop away.
1954 Chum
  plays my Hal.
  His pal
  Crumb
  brays: my Henry.

MAY 17

Dismembering

1950 Hermes has extolled:
  "I like the way you're crazy."
  But we know the world,
  we know the world,
  we know the world.
1951 *Born Yesterday*. Laura
  dismembered my left hand.
  Dick swarmed in my right.
  Honey & venom.
  Popcorn.
1952 Walter files me away in photos,
  casts my face & genitals in plaster,
  shaves my thighs.
  Slowly he is taking me apart,
  making me a part of his collection.
1953 Psychologists might
  nab me, cuff me, book me,
  "Arrested!" But
  they've got
  to catch me first.
1954 Chum's a slim gothic,
  his voice a forest horn.
  He's naturally my prince.
  I can woo Crumb off his ass
  into the meter.

MAY 18

Heresies

1950 Laura sails
  among butterflies,
  scatters with crickets
  & grasshoppers.
  I like the way she's crazy.
1951 When Billie stands up
  to the junkman:
  "Drop Dead!"
  Venus rises
  with pigeons.
1952 Why do I return?
  He has drugged me
  with strange repetitions.
  I serve a ritual
  that must be done.
1953 So much for Oedipus & Everyman.
  Send the crowd home.
  Pack up the masks.
  Let's search our faces.
  Our faces grow more actual every day.
1954 Crumb is the proper
  Humpty Dumpty to be king.
  We can pity his insecurity.
  Our secret hearts
  beat toward the heretic.

MAY 19

Paper Moon

1950 She's had her hair cut short,
wears knickers & a newsboy's cap.
She calls me Mary.
I call her Mike
& I will take her to the prom.
1951 I shared an evening shift
with Dick who'd hid a jug
of Daddy's Red among the hedges.
At midnight in the campus gardens
the moon chinked through our toes like quarters.
1952 At the Sandbar with Bowwow & Lollipop
I drank martinis & sprawled on a grand
with my shirt unbuttoned to the waist:
"It's a Barnum & Bailey world."
Then I threw up beside the highway.
1953 You are not Dixie.
I am not Jack.
Names can't be singular enough.
Any one is queerer
than a category.
1954 Father & son
secure the crown.
"Ripeness is all."
The crowd holds
kingship thrall.

MAY 20

Roars & Whispers

1950 I find myself downtown at ten o'clock.
  Joe's on the air until midnight.
  Mannequins pose important in darkened stores.
  People glide by in private cars.
  A train roars over State Street.
1951 There I was under Moma's red umbrella
  splashing home from work in a spring rain.
  A tiny golden spider dropped from the silk
  rim of the scalloped world & hovered
  at my left ear whispering.
1952 Moma turns up her nose.
  She doesn't think a boy
  should smell so pretty.
  Still she says nothing.
  Dad says less.
1953 Hetero, homo, & bi.
  Peterkin, pumpkin, & pi.
  Bunnies are dumb, foxes sly.
  Nothing's new under the sky.
  Everyone's gone through the rye.
1954 Lilian holds script, my manager.
  Blocking's done. Lines down by Monday.
  Tiger has looted the proproom at Union
  of a crown one can apostrophize: "But thou,
  most fine, hath fed upon the body of my father."

MAY 21

Windows

1950 Windows
   show me the world
   rising transparent,
   a flash in the passing.
   I'm looking in.
1951 We are all reading Rachel Carson's *Sea*.
   Starfish. Likewise, anemone (flowerfish).
   From *anemos*: the wind. Adonis. Adonai.
   Fallen from Heaven. Born on the wind,
   the wave in nature's metaphoricon.
1952 French perfume.
   Peroxide forelock
   whips like palomino
   down the hometown canyons,
   roars like nautilus or nimbus.
1953 What have we from Milton's girls or Shakespeare's?
   Mary Shelley was smart by Percy. What of their boys?
   What matters it that Oscar Wilde had sons?
   Old Socrates would rather die
   than show his wife & kids in public.
1954 Five nights a week
   I'm putting Crumb & Chum
   through Hell: mostly
   iambic pentameter.
   Falstaff's off stage.

MAY 22

Imagining Hermes

1950 The cat takes comfort. As do I.
The golden eye implies the arsenal.
Bright tooth & claw
behind the grin.
Ah! Pussy paw.
1951 So much for Dick & the moon.
I'm his seducer.
He accuses me,
"Even your silences
are intellectual."
1952 Walter's little bitcheries
bubble & build a thousand
animosities. Always
he boils over
at "The Jew."
1953 Who cares a damn for procreation?
Nature's a prodigal: redundant seed!
What's growing must be fed.
What's grown is feed.
Survival's a passing fancy.
1954 I talk to everyone.
There's no one I can talk to.
I imagine Hermes carrying my letter
from the mailbox to the kitchen table.
We have all crossed some unsuspected border.

MAY 23

Farmer in the Dell

1950 How many eaves-
   drop on his air
   waves to me nightly?
   "Jobo to Jackyl.
   Fly me to the moon."

1951 Sybil's gone home to her mother.
   Lew's planting beans for his brother.
   "How you gonna keep him down?"
   Look at me watering her African
   violets. O begonia.

1952 Bowwow is taking a kitten.
   Sybil & Lew. Hot Fudge.
   They'll be ready to leave
   in a week. Mother Cat
   will be mine.

1953 Our actions
   wheel us in: see Ixion.
   Sisyphus under a stone
   mocks married men.
   Genius is something else.

1954 They are married.
   We have set the date.
   The shared troth ought
   to make us closer, not
   four strangers wagging fate.

Des Beaux Gestes

1950 I swipe Joe's levis
off the rumpled sheets.
I put my head in at the waist.
The legs hang sidewise: Jester.
I pull the zipper down my nose.
1951 Laura explains
to Denver & Listerine:
caterpillars have no sex.
"But spiders do,"
adds Jack.
1952 The party continues:
Rex in a chrysanthemum kimono,
Mash in his mantis flesh.
Tricks turn like tumbleweed
through candlelight & Bourbon.
1953 The centaur race.
Genius & Eternity
are different from
intelligence & time.
They have no sex.
1954 I run to Tiger.
He hands me
a dripping comb
of honey which I rake
across his thighs.

MAY 25

Made of No

1950 Then I slip into his sneakers,
  washboard lip & canvas tongue,
  parade the room. Big Man!
  Same game I played
  in Moma's heels & nightgown.
1951 Inflate the clock
  & let it float
  to the moon.
  Abolish every creed
  & make heart room.
1952 Knowing is sin.
  Christopher,
  keeping track,
  won't speak
  to Jack.
1953 Sex involves.
  Genius dissolves.
  Eternity: old lamp.
  There's the rub'll
  get a lad in trouble.
1954 Tigerlily
  & Saint Simpleton.
  What are little joys
  made of? Made of
  no thing. Nothing.

MAY 26

Bodies

1950 I don't skip school anymore.
   Joe moves to Syracuse.
   Tomorrow's our last
   Saturday. Parting's
   such sweating sorrow.
1951 Give me a cake
   & tell me I can't eat it.
   I've news for you.
   I'll eat my cake
   & have it too.
1952 Body of Laura.
   Walter & Bowwow.
   Sybil & Lew.
   My sullen flesh.
   The body of the world.
1953 I've lost
   interest in argument.
   Tech tonight for *Phoenix*.
   Lilian's Freida Lawrence.
   Good like bread.
1954 The king is sick
   & weary is the prince.
   He comes from the night & Falstaff
   into this lighted room.
   The dear heart's dumb & dark.

MAY 27

Music in Another Room

1950 We picnic on the floor,
Murphy's stripped mattress ticking.
We take the luggage down & dare
to stand together on the curb,
waiting for a taxi.
1951 Reading *Brideshead Revisited*
at the station.
Expecting Sybil,
next train.
The next train didn't come.
1952 My sullen flesh
accepts the lewd caress
of lover or tall grass
until I waken: nothing
but a swarm of bees.
1953 I know
bread rises.
I'm not
so sure about
the phoenix.
1954 The king asleep.
Hal finds a golden crown.
There's music in another room.
There'll be an interview & then
a brother will arrive from battle.

MAY 28

I'll Sit Again Through Phoenix

1950 Moma believes
I saved my pennies
to buy this Smith-Corona,
grey with pea-green keys.
Joe's gift. Joe's gone.
1951 Sybil found me at dawn
asleep on the wooden bench,
my sandals stolen.
Barefoot I walked her home
crowing, "Waugh! Waugh!"
1952 "Watch me emerge
from the tunnel
with my lovers
& a kitten."
Supernumerary.
1953 I'll sit again through *Phoenix*
to take Lily to her dorm.
She will be Frieda still
in make-up & costume,
not to miss curfew.
1954 Night & a music & a war
circumscribe the body of the king.
We sound the deep
of his eternal
dream.

MAY 29

Hovering

1950 The Smith-Corona weight between us
served for gravity.
Then he let go
& sailed away
leaving me anchored.
1951 "Sebastian embodies
our later-day Roman Catholic:
rotten & unrepentant."
I leave Sybil at her door,
wade home through dewy Saint Panther's.
1952 Imagination
entertains
quaint oppositions:
train & kitten,
kitten & train.
1953 Greyhound
transports me
to Ithaca
where Laura
waits among hills.
1954 Concentrate, Chum,
on where you're coming from.
Think Poins & fat Sir Jack
until they hover.
The audience will duck from bats.

MAY 30

Round

1950 At 33 revs
  per minute
  it was not
  such a merry
  go round.
1951 Hermes & I
  went to see *M.*
  I mean no harm.
  Why do I identify
  with killers?
1952 The train runs round
  a cardboard scenery.
  The kitten catches it
  coming through a tunnel,
  derails it with a paw.
1953 The bus was late
  owing to rain & miles
  of muddy detour.
  I got off at the campus.
  She fretted downtown.
1954 Beer & sandwiches with Lil.
  The jukebox bubbles "Ebbtide."
  The waitress is ready
  as an ogre's wife
  to hide us in the oven.

MAY 31

Belonging to No One

1950 I'll go.
  I'll go to bed.
  I'll go to bed tonight.
  I'll go to bed tonight alone.
  I'll go to bed tonight alone & sleep.
1951 "Little boy,
  little girl,
  come ride
  my big truck
  to Never-Never."
1952 Saint Panther's pond
  lies among dusty weeds.
  The sunlight dusts its darkness.
  Laura shows me how to kill
  a butterfly doing no damage.
1953 I found the dorm she named me in her letter
  & my dorm-mate for the weekend,
  her roommate's Bo,
  all knee & elbow
  & grey eye.
1954 *The Sun Also Rises.*
  A bottle of wine.
  I drifted down a Sunday afternoon
  among the dandelions
  belonging to no one.

JUNE 1

A Kitten Sleeping

1950 Hermes is the boy with ears
  like winged sandals.
  He does not ask for lies.
  We prowl together
  down the broken tower.
1951 The child must die:
  talking to strangers, parents,
  taking a nickel,
  a lemondrop, a ride,
  a helping hand.
1952 Bowwow & Lollipop
  are on that train.
  The kitten slept
  in my Sunday lap
  on B's clean handkerchief.
1953 Grey eyes
  absorb the weekend
  make believe: prom on the
  mountain, picnic in the
  hollow, Laura, hollow.
1954 In Tiger's room
  I dream of his return:
  Papa's porridge,
  Mama's rocker,
  Goldilocks.

JUNE 2

Thresholds

1950 Hermes appeared in English,
World History & Plane Geometry.
We queued up to get textbooks,
met by chance between huge double doors,
wagged together to the bus.
1951 *The Turn of the Screw.*
The world is governess,
respectable, ignorant. Good
women exorcise
our innocence.
1952 Hot Fudge dubbed, "Muff!"
christening deliverance at once.
We shared the burden up & down Manhattan.
Hermes blew, "Huff!" & "Puff!" Theresa.
I fell in love with love.
1953 In Syracuse I look
up Joe in the phone book.
What would he say
if I called?
"Egg Salad Sandwich."
1954 Herr Brain offers to drive me home.
I take him to meet Tiger.
We find his room teeming
with brief boys.
Tiger, on dirty laundry, picks his nose.

JUNE 3

Met Among the Enemy

1950 We met among the enemy.
    I thought him funny.
    He must have thought me dumb.
    But Hermes is the boy
    who shapes my song.
1951 Each freak acts out
    the killer impulse
    of the universe:
    our hearts,
    my heart.
1952 "A-round the corner
    B-neath the berry tree,
    A-round the corner,
    B-neath the bush
    looking for" you & me.
1953 We shared a green bench
    at the edge of elm
    shade & sunlight
    & I trilled, "Lil, will
    you be my girl?"
1954 Herr Brain
    disapproved.
    The Judge
    reigns King
    of the Dead.

JUNE 4

Bogeyman

1950 He is terrible.
  I only laugh
  but he is terrible.
  Flowers know the rain
  is terrible.
1951 Poor Queen.
  Painfully gentle Bogeyman,
  sad-eyed as dog or cow.
  Monster & child merge. Housel
  of our fear & rage.
1952 Lollipop at Horn & Hardart
  waited for a cup
  to unfold from the spigot
  while his coffee
  ran away.
1953 "Lilian, be my girl.
  I will be your guy."
  All our hands,
  a tangled skein,
  graced my poor knees.
1954 I would rather be
  actor than director.
  From the backrow
  I watch among shadows.
  My puppets writhe.

JUNE 5

Muddy Paws

1950 He brings me
the big world.
I give him
my emptiness
to fill.

1951 Laura always chatters at passing dogs,
remarks on the weather, asks about
their health & families & where they've been,
compliments their tails or muddy paws.
They look a little shy.

1952 We missed our excursion
trying to get Lollipop sober
& Bowwow had to buy us
tickets on a later run.
Good lover. Good friend.

1953 A guy & a girl:
common as apples,
simple as God at the core.
I won't be graceless
anymore.

1954 The aftermath of mass
& masque: cast party.
Crumb like Mr Peanut
escorts Miss Cashew.
Everyone's engaged.

JUNE 6

Goldberg Variations

1950 Sidney, kiddo
  I thought I knew,
  took me aside
  to warn me.
  "That Hermes is a Jew."
1951 I look back
  to my notes for a novel.
  They promise life.
  Life dies
  in the writing.
1952 Wanda Landowska lifts
  The Goldberg Variations off her keyboard
  like cutting a diamond.
  The mind's geometry
  facets sky & sea.
1953 I shall win
  free of the past.
  Lilian shelters me
  like trees or a tall
  ship sailing.
1954 Dame Agnes commended me
  for having rid Chum of affection.
  I tuned him in
  to Shakespeare's singing.
  The music worked.

JUNE 7

Only Music

1950 After God fell
  & we drove him from the garden,
  what was left to do? Explore
  the planet, seize the day,
  invent religion.
1951 *Misunderstood:*
  A Novel.
  There can be
  no point of view.
  No one is narrator.
1952 Only music comprehends.
  I am trying to get it
  into my head & body.
  Rhythm risen to design
  sounds the word.
1953 We drive out of town,
  stop at a grassy slope
  where a doe & fawn
  step into the forest
  shedding our disbelief.
1954 Exams begin.
  The college year packs up,
  scatters toward the shore,
  a hometown job,
  a summer's boredom.

JUNE 8

Gospels

1950 Hamilton's *Mythology*
gives me new gods
whose glamour,
lust & redundance
educe me.
1951 Everyone
judges
everyone.
What is a mind
to make up?
1952 A hummingbird
buzzes about
a bud, a bawd,
an immanent business
like God.
1953 Hermes arrives.
I have written to Sybil & Lew
the news: gospel
of my engagement.
1954 We study together
for finals at her dorm:
a livingroom
shaded by looming
chestnut.

JUNE 9

The Flow

1950 Hera, Zeus & Aphrodite.
Artemis, Pan, Apollo.
Ares & Dionysus. Hermes:
messenger & friend.
The winged foot.
1951 Ignorant rumor
is my theme. Watch all
the world conform
to reputation in the hall of fame.
1952 I am amazed
so poor a fool as Walter
could have enspelled me.
My flesh bleeds clean
to welcome Hermes home.
1953 I come from the john.
My morning bath
gurgles down the drain
like birdsong: "Here's my son."
Take away the stone.
1954 Her sisters haul
strange luggage down the stair.
Their passage turns the gloom
to aviary or
aquarium.

JUNE 10

Wind & a Wake

1950 My Hermes walks
so fast he makes the wind.
I'm swept along behind his magic carpet,
a fistful of bright fringe
in my left hand.
1951 We wouldn't dare
to be or even seem
different.
Who would disturb
the easy dream?
1952 I made a terminal scene.
I was not clever. "Walter,
take the dirty pictures
you have made of me & stick them
up your ass." That's justice.
1953 Science continually
alters my identity:
new star in the sky
or fossil unicorn
or me at the busstop waiting.
1954 Hermes will not come again.
After many
& many
a summer,
Hermes moves on.

JUNE 11

A Music Covering Our Voices

1950 What a lot of walking we have done!
    What a lot of sitting in his blue
    & yellow room! at the top
    of the stair with the door closed,
    music covering our voices.
1951 Scene from the novel: Sidney at prayer.
    Abashed by God's impersonality
    he turns to Satan,
    but no one will woo
    the devil away from Jack.
1952 He was appalled by my vulgarity.
    I've never been so happy
    to be me: common
    Jack Bean
    of Bung Hole.
1953 Aiming Henry J
    up country roads
    Lilian sings me
    the German songs
    she grew up on.
1954 I will go down with Lilian
    to Brooklyn & Long Island
    Sunday morning.
    One last exam banishes spring.
    Summer resurges.

JUNE 12

The Man on Saxophone

1950 So I took Laura
  to the Junior Prom
  & flirted with the man
  on saxophone
  while we danced.
1951 Miss Shrimp won't live in words:
  her sleeplessness,
  aversions & bitchery.
  Nobody believes
  case histories.
1952 Hermes returns. Theresa
  turns with him. Hot Fudge
  calls from Connecticut
  putting her Muff on the phone.
  Puss in glass slippers.
1953 We have a weekend
  before Lilian heads home.
  With Hermes at Howard Johnson,
  we have to meet each other newly.
  I have a girl.
1954 We're parked
  on some sidestreet
  in Albany.
  "Lilian, wait.
  I want a wedding night."

JUNE 13

Our Music Like a Raft

1950 Holy Spirit.
  I wafted homeward
  alone at dawn
  & heard the first
  bird sing.
1951 Lew's back
  at Sybil's
  baking bread,
  writing stories.
  Sun bursts the turned earth.
1952 Hermestheresa on the sofa.
  Me on the floor
  reading to them: poems
  & the novel. Mom & Dad
  asleep in the back bedroom.
1953 We laugh at "Old Cape Cod."
  "Little things mean a lot."
  Ubiquitous Hit Parade
  drifts above our music
  like a raft.
1954 It isn't really
  downhill all
  the way. I
  only think so
  watching the map.

JUNE 14

Watching the Traffic

1950 What is art?
A feeble joke about Picasso.
The solemn observation:
"Artists get rich & famous
when they're dead."
1951 On Sunday I graduate
with Hermes & Miss Shrimp
& Denver. They will go
to college in the fall.
What will I do?
1952 We drive to Saratoga.
On boarding house porches
old women rock
& watch the traffic
knitting.
1953 Tomorrow morning
Lilian departs.
We clung together
in the ignorant hot night.
My watch stopped.
1954 We find our way
to Saint James Place.
Hermes & Miriam show us
sketches of the probable
expected child.

JUNE 15

Nobody Watches the Movie

1950 Art is not mean.
It knows no moderation.
Good for nothing,
it is good
for me.
1951 Is there a herdsman
who meaning well
will take me in
or give me away
to some unsuspecting royalty?
1952 I play with Theresa's
bracelets in the back seat.
Nobody watches the movie.
Star after star
gets shot.
1953 I have been
a pretty little thing,
a slender glittering thing,
perilous Tinker Ding-Dong,
fatal to moths & flies.
1954 The boys are
happy to be boys.
The girls are
happy to be girls.
The foetus isn't kicking.

JUNE 16

Kiss Me

1950 Some saints wave,
some makers mock:
Degas, Cezanne,
Lautrec, Van Gogh,
Gaugin.
1951 At the madhouse
rehearsal for graduation
as I crossed the stage
some fellow shouted, "Kiss me."
I pinned him down & did.
1952 We found an unlikely saloon
tended by somebody's Polish *babka*.
A player piano honky-tonked.
Above the bar, in sepia,
a spotted cow exuded.
1953 I am supposed
to be looking for a summer job.
I arrive at the door of some shop
& the sweat of my armpits & crotch
washes me away from asking.
1954 Going for mustard
to a corner store,
I minced on my imagined heels
pursuing Hermes' fabled stride.
Maybe we didn't need to speak.

JUNE 17

Enormous Key Unwinding

1950 Walking the broken tracks
  to dead ends of old Erie
  mucked with algae slime & milkweed.
  "Laura, Hermes, we should not
  love beauty & virtue only."
1951 I was granted
  my diploma today
  to a stunning
  ovation.
  Moma was deeply moved.
1952 Tanner has arranged for my promotion.
  I will keep Science & Technology in order
  at a little raise in pay.
  County Public pipes my way
  toward fall & American State.
1953 I dream
  about Lilian
  mothering
  my children.
  Choose time.
1954 We watched a sidewalk hawker
  demonstrate a toy:
  a painted metal ship
  with painted metal sails,
  enormous key unwinding.

JUNE 18

Vegetable Acts

1950 The milkweed pods
  like ugly sisters' feet
  eventually release
  silk seeds to the breeze-borne
  season of their fancy.
1951 The crowd
  clapped
  their respect.
  They didn't dare
  a clearer mockery.
1952 Hermes has painted Job.
  Sitting in ashes
  the old man prays
  wrapped in a lovely web,
  waiting for spiders.
1953 A local A&P
  employs me after all.
  I'll pack brown bags
  & save my money
  for the fall.
1954 I act
  the fool
  falling
  upon Lilian,
  awkward as a tree.

JUNE 19

Sensible Shoes

1950 Laura is best
  outdoors. The open
  field just fits her:
  wilderness rooted
  in sensible shoes.
1951 I filled out applications at GE.
  I couldn't seem to understand the questions.
  I have some lovely answers
  but I couldn't find the blanks
  to put them in.
1952 Old Job did very well
  (I've looked him up) until
  his friends arrived to watch.
  We meet by daylight.
  Should I curse God?
1953 This ninety-cent an hour drudgery
  provides a room off campus
  for my sophomore year.
  I'll have my books & records
  & Lilian. Meals out.
1954 The girls shoo
  the superfluous males
  out of the kitchen
  & lay again the table
  we have laid.

JUNE 20

God's Love

1950 Her flight behind the net's
a very gamut. She never
steps in cowshit,
leaves each moony pie
for maundy me.
1951 I got lost of course
seeking my way out of the hive
onto the boulevard. Hot pavement
waved with june bugs on their backs.
"I do not think that they will wave to me."
1952 I love
God's love
of everything
he's made: the moon
& elephants' sinewed stones.
1953 To Lew & Sybil:
"Aberration is conformity.
Old women swooned, 'He ought to be a girl!'
No one ever doubted I was queer."
Now Lew thinks I'm his fault.
1954 Hermes & Miriam came with us.
Lilian's dad
burst from the door
shouting into the garden,
"Mutter! Och Gott! Der kinder!"

JUNE 21

What Dad Said

1950 She climbs a tree.
   We attend
   at the root.
   Hermes engorges
   a mushroom.
1951 "Those june bugs ought
   to join the union,"
   says my dad.
   I spy a battled
   sorrow in his eyes.
1952 "When the morning stars
   sang together, where
   were you? Doth the hawk
   fly by wisdom?
   Gird thy loins."
1953 Dear Lew, the world
   made me & I had fallen
   before you came
   & brought me
   the new world.
1954 Lilian's dad danced
   to Miriam's pregnancy.
   "Clean your plate.
   Like a cow
   you must get fat."

JUNE 22

Nobody Home

1950 Laura & the leaves
discover whisper,
whip & whistle.
What the world
might be!
1951 Mom at the other
end of the table
scans the want ads.
"Moma, is it time
to sell the cow?"
1952 Sybil & Lew have got married.
Christopher invited me to play tennis.
The courts were all taken.
We wandered toward Sybil's.
Nobody home.
1953 I must
convince
myself
we are
real.
1954 Her mother comes from the garden.
Wonderful shoes!
The shape of nursery rhymes
& full of holes
where bawling brats hang out.

JUNE 23

Snaps

1950 Three city rats
   play treehouse:
   Tarzan & Jane,
   puer ex machina.
   A brownie snaps.
1951 Two bookstores serve
   the sprawling town.
   Best Sellers. Rare Editions.
   Slow doors exhaled behind me.
   Neither is hiring.
1952 We met them ascending
   the stairs as we rolled
   rattling down.
   Champagne & lilies
   of the valley.
1953 Our acts
   have consequences.
   It makes
   some difference
   what I do.
1954 She pretends
   to be ashamed
   of her soiled apron,
   hangs it on a nail
   in the garage.

JUNE 24

Maybe I Am Not a Fool

1950 I hear them
   in the woods
   & weeds.
   I lurk
   beside Mohawk.
1951 Lew spins the sunshine on his finger.
   "Let's run away." He herds me aboard a bus
   that jerks us to his brother's farm.
   We splash away our troubles
   in an honest swimming hole.
1952 Suddenly they're married.
   I manage not to speak
   about betrayal. We ignore
   our loneliness. Maybe
   I am not a fool.
1953 I write & save my money.
   I'm avoiding Laura.
   To be honest,
   she called me once
   & has not called again.
1954 We packed a lunch
   & took it to Jones Beach.
   Hermes & I changed
   to strops & trunks
   in Gentlemen's.

JUNE 25

What Hermes Said

1950 "Green is a warm color,"
   said Hermes. & Laura,
   "Trees have good manners."
   Bean Sprout
   fell out.
1951 We roasted dogs
   & spuds in silver foil.
   His nephews sank my loafers in the lake.
   The family went to their beds. He browned
   me underwater & we drowned.
1952 The best is Sybil's
   got a job in Brooklyn.
   The worst is me
   still left behind
   stupidly waiting my turn.
1953 Hermes brought wine.
   We sat on the swayback porch
   swigging cheap Burgundy.
   Shrimp danced an octopus shimmy.
   I've never seen Mom & Dad so entertained.
1954 We burned
   except Miriam.
   Hermes huddled in towels
   & umbrella shade.
   I hummed with salt & sand.

JUNE 26

Metamorphoses

1950 The earth turns
  greener every day.
  The animal still
  must fall to vine & flower.
  Only the vegetable is real.
1951 The family at breakfast couldn't know
  that we were still an otter
  tangled among pondlily stems & stones.
  The bus, a medicine man's rattle,
  accepted our remains.
1952 A wedding gift.
  We found a relic toaster.
  "This should have been a birdcage,"
  said Laura. Said Lew,
  "To toast a tit."
1953 They have had Lady
  put to sleep.
  She has borne
  too many babies
  & gone blind.
1954 "The sea is there."
  I raked the sand
  spinning off
  the nakedness at hand.
  The sea was there.

JUNE 27

Animal Vegetable

1950 Only the vegetable is real:
   Hermes Gillyflower; Laura Sorghum.
   I am the orphic Iris
   that grows on the moon:
   Iridaceae.
1951 Lew seems the same.
   No pearls.
   No coral.
   Nothing of him fades
   or suffers a pond change.
1952 Hermes brought them
   Mozart: O! LP.
   We made an altar
   of good things
   with wildflowers & wine.
1953 We are
   keeping
   one of her
   litter:
   Tom.
1954 I rode some waves.
   The ocean
   is big
   enough
   for me.

JUNE 28

What Jack Said

1950 Joe was to write me
care of County Public.
A month has passed.
Sex was a substitute
for rest & poetry.
1951 When we got off the bus
Lew said, "I think
I'll grow a beard."
He wants to wag
like goats.
1952 Bowwow provided
angel food & drove.
Lew deviled eggs
& the rain wanted
to prevent our holiday.
1953 "Tom won't be any kind of pet
unless you have him fixed."
I only know my feet
& muscles ache
from cans & bags.
1954 Everybody saw me off.
The train wagged.
I'm riding backward
but the river
is no fool.

JUNE 29

What the Bells Said

1950 Saint John the Divine.
    Between the convent & the church
    a formal lawn with yew & ginkgo.
    Nuns & pigeons share this interim
    with bell sound.
1951 I got home
    to find the Board of Regents
    offers me a scholarship.
    Mom & Dad have been
    opening my mail again.
1952 I said something fresh
    & Bowwow slapped my face.
    Lew & Sybil approved.
    The wheels sang over the pavement.
    How abrupt the lesson is!
1953 Castration is not a proper subject
    for Sunday dinner conversation. I admit
    I'll miss that white-rose knot,
    like Puck in tights,
    a fur impertinence.
1954 I hang
    upon the gate.
    Saint Simpleton,
    posthumous me,
    awaits burial.

JUNE 30

Lucy Church

1950 I made a poem
  of that bell space.
  Nuns & pigeons
  come & go
  tolling Armageddon.
1951 The State
  will pay tuition,
  books & busfare.
  Will the University
  accept me?
1952 We parked
  beside Lake George,
  a pterodactyl, & ate
  our picnic in Bowwow's
  drumming convertible.
1953 Hermes reads Willa Cather.
  I'm with Stein. *Death Comes
  to the Archbishop, Lucy
  Church Amiably,*
  amiably.
1954 Lilian & I discovered William Morris
  windows at the Episcopal Cathedral in Albany.
  Impossible to believe such colors,
  so profound a green
  could cross Atlantic.

JULY 1

Webster

1950 I call the churchyard
poem *Armageddon*.
Pomme. That's what
I opened to in *Webster*.
Pomme de terror.
1951 Burden & Miss Blazes
recommend me
to Dean Spoke.
I've an appointment:
Thursday the Fifth.
1952 Goodbye!
My fancy,
if we go
anywhere,
we'll go.
1953 *Lectures in America.*
Three Lives. My Antonia.
Youth and the Bright Medusa.
I found out Medusa
is a jellyfish.
1954 I read.
I read
& I write.
I am bored. Routine
is good. *Root. Rut.*

JULY 2

Don't Tell

1950 No one will ever know
how torture & despair
made up the fee
I had to pay
for that gay *pomme.*
1951 How will I get through
the interview?
Shall I tell
about Murphy & my truant
days with Joe?
1952 They're gone.
Lew's brother's little truck
rattled them away to Brooklyn.
I waved goodbye.
'Twarn't nuttin' else to do.
1953 At work
cashiers & clerks
stare down my lunch
& dinner hour book:
Gide's *If It Die.*
1954 Tiger has gone home.
He left me a present
in Moma's keeping
wrapped in an evening
Star. I see stars.

JULY 3

Boy Blue

1950 Sad *pommes*
cost less.
Boy Blue,
sad pomps
are easy.
1951 I will say,
"Miss Spoke, I suffered
severe depression.
I was a running joke
& sick a lot."
1952 I am water.
I fall & flow.
I am water
but I cut no
channel.
1953 It's heavy work.
I will
develop muscles:
majuscule & morbid
clams.
1954 *Four Saints*
on old 78's
& a second-hand edition
of *Jerusalem Delivered*,
warped & olive brown.

JULY 4

Listening to the World

1950 Mr & Mrs Pimpernel
include me,
Laura's little friend,
in their family holiday,
surrounded on all sides by water.
1951 "I got in
with a bad
crowd,
but I have seen
the error of my ways."
1952 Baudelaire's *Intimate Journals:*
"If you are no true men,
be at least true animals."
But, on the other hand,
the dandy's careful glove.
1953 I figure
(four from nine)
it's going on
fifteen years
since I buried anything.
1954 Saint Simple listens to the world.
Two little girls
on opposing porches
taunt across
a vaunted avenue.

JULY 5

America

1950 Lake George.
  Our holiday sunburns
  bless America
  The waves & rocks
  have come to bed with me.
1951 I sat
  in the waitingroom
  till noon.
  At last the student aide
  invited me to lunch.
1952 Bowwow has asked me to wear
  his grandmother's wedding ring.
  Embossed with rosebuds & a rim
  of love-knots it exactly fits
  my little finger.
1953 Packing bags
  for the girls at checkout:
  "Never put the beer
  or toilet paper
  on the top."
1954 I'm going swimming.
  "You are not."
  I'm going downtown.
  "You are not."
  I'm going to gramma's.

JULY 6

Lewd Embrace

1950 The water from the boat
  looks about a foot
  deep. Step out,
  you never reach rock;
  only the ice-age shock.
1951 I confided I had to pee.
  Jesse showed me to the men's room.
  I stood close: poor Weepy Wee.
  He hauled a side of beef
  out of the locker.
1952 Novella: trace
  an affair
  from lewd embrace
  to companionship
  tender & genuine.
1953 Those vulgar girls.
  Those vulgar girls.
  Vulgar is.
  Grace is.
  Vulgarity is saving grace.
1954 The ritual
  holy moly:
  "You are not."
  I'm going
  to Heaven.

JULY 7

Dreaming Under Evergreen

1950 Mountains lift off the lake
a massive sleep of pleistocene
dreaming under evergreen,
dreaming of water & clean stone,
dreaming of us lithesome & alive.
1951 Dean Spoke politely nodded
over all the nice letters, grandly yawned
over my grades. At 3:30 in the afternoon
(I'd arrived promptly at 9:00) she looked
at me. Asked why I had done so poorly.
1952 "Greek democracy became
a hatred and a horror
of leadership
annihilating its elite,
condemning its best men."
1953 They pay us in cash.
The neatly sealed, narrow
brown envelopes
remind me
of fly paper.
1954 I listen.
Still a third little girl
says nothing.
Not "Me too."
Not "Boohoo."

JULY 8

Turning to Stone

1950 We lay on our backs
   & let the water
   swarming up the rocks
   wash over us
   holding our breath.
1951 "I was bored," I said.
   It wasn't the right answer I'm afraid
   because she looked at me some more,
   looked at the window, looked at me again.
   I tried hard but couldn't turn to stone.
1952 From C. G. Jung: The ego
   is surrounded by & rests
   on consciousness & is concerned
   with adjustment
   to external reality.
1953 I tuck each envelope
   into a bureau drawer
   asking my arms
   & feet to wait
   until September.
1954 Hazelton Spencer's *British Lit*
   is bigger than both of us.
   "You & who else?"
   Also I've found
   my First Communion book.

JULY 9

The Passing Content

1950 We slip from stone
   into the pool: we'd think
   we were angels or eels
   except for the hair
   & water in our eyes.
1951 She would promise me very little.
   If I go back to school & show some skill
   in Latin, math & science, the college will
   accept me next year. This means
   I'll have to win a scholarship again.
1952 I conclude the ego is a fool.
   "A function is a form of psychic action
   which remains the same whatever
   its passing content." Such functions are
   thought, feeling & sensation, intuition.
1953 Gertrude writes about Picasso & Matisse,
   a little crowd creating
   a new world.
   Then Hemingway shows up.
   Cocteau.
1954 There it lay:
   a june bug
   at the bottom of a box
   full of odd trash.
   Prayer book.

JULY 10

A Great Conch

1950 We had an island to ourselves:
wildflowers & white birch.
Lichens & ferns & mosses.
Laura knows all their names.
She goes unerring to each insect nursery.
1951 I'll do it.
Sybil & Lew chortled about my day
with the dean & her gay aide.
Their joy for me lays the future
between my ears like a great conch.
1952 "Thinking and feeling
are both rational.
One or the other must rule."
What do I think of Bowwow,
for instance, & how do I feel?"
1953 I wrestle restless.
Imperatives announce:
matter lies there,
potential line & color.
The word lurks.
1954 Little black book provides the Mass,
the Stations of the Cross,
& sentimental pictures: boy & girl
hold hands on a bridge & angels
dote about their heads.

JULY 11

Everyone & Everybody

1950 A day in the sun
I can't let go.
Eternity:
where everyone
likes everybody.
1951 I'll let the institution
have its way remembering
"perfection does not move
to punish
or reward."
1952 *"Persona*
is a compromise between
the individual and reality."
The mask mocks:
personality.
1953 The universe
is uncreated.
We must be
the word & make
the world.
1954 Angels & devils.
Pigeons & crows.
I will be
nobody's fault
but my own.

JULY 12

Loveletters

1950 Driftwood or leaf
  turned white & hard
  with mineral deposit.
  Everything seemed.
  Everything was.
1951 Lew's beard
  takes shape from stubble.
  Sybil & I study
  A Pictorial History of Hair
  trying to like the idea.
1952 Keats said the poet
  has no character.
  One thing I know:
  I don't know
  what I'm doing.
1953 Words burn
  our flesh: old log
  or old loveletter.
  Exquisite is ash!
  I tremble so to wait.
1954 My sneakers suck
  & slap wet pavement
  blotting neon,
  shaping Priapus
  out of shadow.

JULY 13

O Gertrude, Intercede for Me

1950 Wind rattles my window
  & I do not understand.
  The bulb in my lamp is buzzing.
  What does it want to say?
  I run out into the rain.
1951 Jesse surprised me getting off work
  & took me to a bar & bought me Scotch
  & gave me a lot of mean advice.
  He made a trip & spent his money
  to tell me I HAD BETTER LEARN TO WALK.
1952 Attitudes.
  Introvert or extrovert:
  vertibrate or crustacean.
  I gather it matters
  how I wear my spine.
1953 Ashes to ashes,
  art to art.
  O Alice B!
  O Gertrude,
  intercede for me.
1954 The armoring of Sir Gawain,
  before he leaves King Arthur
  to seek the green foe, is a burial.
  He is laid away in metal, fur, embroidery:
  love & labor of all hands.

JULY 14

The Blood in my Shoes

1950 I thought about throwing
   my books out. It was better
   to go in sandals & a sweatshirt
   & stand there looking in at the window.
   The rain wouldn't do me any harm.
1951 My fourth-grade teacher told me that.
   Four hundred kids have told me everyday.
   So who the hell is Jesse!
   I wiggle. God forgive me.
   I had better learn to walk.
1952 "It's very difficult
   to designate a person's type.
   This is most true
   of the artist who
   has emptied the deep."
1953 Hermes & I
   go hiking and discover
   a house of breath:
   whispering farmstead
   of sighs & broken hints.
1954 I am guilty of everything.
   Nighthawk & bat
   & the blood in my shoes.
   How shall I love life
   until September?

JULY 15

Repression

1950 *You and Psychiatry,*
   Menninger & Leaf:
   a human child passes
   through three phases.
   Solar. Lunar. Terrestrial.
1951 Lew & Hermes undertake
   my instruction: largely a matter
   of keeping one's feet about a foot apart.
   "As if you had a basketball
   between your thighs."
1952 A Personal Unconscious.
   What is a little P U made of?
   Emotion.
   Repression.
   Memory.
1953 Behind the peeling primrose,
   plaster & hair; behind the crumbled
   plaster, slats & dust & newspaper
   insulation selling horses
   & corsets. Whalebone stays.
1954 Elizabethan sonnets
   sing me to sleep.
   Spenser & Marlowe.
   Malory: everybody dies.
   I'm out all night.

JULY 16

The Silence of the Cemetery Pond

1950 The body is sexual. So are all its actions.
   The mouth is the sucking center of the universe.
   Learning begins in the ass: a place for everything.
   Lo! there's the little pet.
   They also serve who only stand and wait.
1951 "Remember the earth
   is not eggs.
   You needn't float.
   You are not Cinderella
   or a serpent."
1952 Collective unconscious:
   eruptions from the deep, the past.
   Depthless, timeless kaleidoscope.
   I think how orange carp
   silence the cemetery pond.
1953 Someone, however, swept the debris
   into a corner of each room:
   rags of lace curtain,
   doll's head with a winking eye,
   a *Book of Common Prayer*.
1954 The station john: hang out.
   Or hang outside some grim
   gay bar. Jack Sprat
   will eat it fat
   or lean.

JULY 17

Stampede

1950 Oedipus Everyman.
  Wouldn't it be fun to murder Daddy?
  We toss his genitals
  into Moma's bath. Unrivaled
  Venus rises from the sea.
1951 "Swing your shoulders.
  Hold those hips."
  I'm wind-up Frankenstein.
  No wonder men are dolts: stampede
  is all they've time to think about.
1952 "Consciousness aims always at adjustment
  of the individual to the external world.
  Unconsciousness, indifferent to this goal,
  has all the impersonality of nature."
  Mountain, flower, shark. Don't care.
1953 In broken china one
  grubby hand, missing a thumb.
  The cotton body
  in another room
  with patent leather shoes.
1954 *Give me my scallop-shell of quiet.*
  Sweet Themmes runne softly
  till I end my song.
  Run soft until I end my long life
  in tigerlily season.

JULY 18

The Maze at Crete

1950 Murder & incest
  feed the root.
  Don't eat
  that carrot,
  Proserpine!
1951 Sybil behind her desk at County P
  observes me at work,
  congratulates my swagger.
  I'd like to cry.
  So would she.
1952 Eruptions from the deep:
  mute & ambiguous archetype.
  I am the maze at Crete.
  Theseus & bull & Ariadne.
  O Hermaphrodite!
1953 Old farmhouse
  beside the older
  river brings
  the unremembered family
  to mindless dust.
1954 Saint Simple says burn
  to the legend.
  Privacy.
  Poetry.
  Fidelity.

JULY 19

Don't Sit under the Appletree

1950 Sigmund is clever
  but I never
  repressed the daily murder of my father.
  I've also thought he might be lots of fun
  in a shed or apple shade.
1951 Now that I have learned
  to act the male,
  I'll hang him in a closet
  to haul out
  on suitable occasions.
1952 The cross.
  Peter & Magdalene.
  I'd like to have been that one centurion
  who knew what was happening:
  "Truly this was the son."
1953 Each orchard crotch
  darkens with caterpillar
  tents, Hermes.
  "Hermes, Hermes,
  let's get out of here."
1954 Legend enforces privacy.
  It serves two ways:
  it neither gives nor takes.
  The legend simply stays.
  We must bury our gods.

JULY 20

Best Man

1950 The little fellow
   at the crossroads
   raped the old man
   & went on to be queen.
   Jocasta is a drag.
1951 I've got myself a lady.
   The neighbors mistreated her.
   I rescued.
   She is white & mews,
   nibbles my approximate nipples.
1952 At last I understand the chorus:
   Collective Consciousness.
   Full of talk & worry,
   understanding nothing,
   the farce of common sense.
1953 Hermes raves about Ben Shahn.
   "The Jewish artists are the best today
   because they are not afraid
   to show some feeling
   in their work."
1954 September first
   will be my wedding day.
   It is not far away.
   Hermes will enact
   best man.

JULY 21

Lady is Enough

1950 I missed my latency.
  Marty was largely
  the instrument
  of my untimely passion.
  Also, unripe Pandora.
1951 I like to watch her in the window
  while the sunlight through her ears
  illuminates the tracery of veins.
  I'd dub her Celeste.
  The family says Lady is enough.
1952 "Woman is the bridge to the unconscious."
  Grandmother Raven coughing up her crow.
  Sybil's chignon in the rain.
  Mostly, mostly Laura
  showing me her bugs.
1953 Finally I spoke to Laura as we sat
  together in the college gardens.
  She said, "I knew you'd come around someday
  to women. I always knew: it won't be me."
  Then she stood up & walked away.
1954 Somewhere,
  distant as a star,
  distant as snowfall,
  I will replace my past
  with Lilian.

JULY 22

A Butterfly Dreaming

1950 Moma waited on a balcony.
  I sailed through a garden
  & a midnight air. She bloomed.
  I entered & was utterly assumed.
  I woke to my first wet dream.
1951 She's perched on the toilet seat
  to watch me take my bath.
  She sets to her own preening
  to teach me what her mom
  taught her: a better way.
1952 I spend my afternoons in Hermes' bed.
  He's painting me.
  I'm naked to the waist.
  The rest is crazy quilt.
  He's painting me asleep.
1953 So that was Laura
  in the end. A young woman
  swinging a pair of sandals,
  gradual among trees,
  slipping from dumb fingers.
1954 Everything is.
  Everything is going.
  Everything is going to be.
  Everything is going to be all
  right.

JULY 23

Parables

1950 "Consciousness is
an open drawer."
The world is a locker room.
Grab bag fruits the loom.
Catch all!
1951 She goes about it slow
& voluptuous until
she comes to clean between her toes;
savagely rips the old hunt
& heart out of her moonbeam claws.
1952 He's over there
behind the easel
chattering his head
off the canvas
hoping to catch mine.
1953 I'm writing a story about Rapunzel,
a girl who, being her own witch mother,
withdraws into a lighthouse tower.
But Richard Prince, appearing from the sea,
invades her solitude & brings her back to life.
1954 Tiger writes me parables
about his garden.
"Blackberries
grow unruly
but they blossom white."

JULY 24

Pulling Weeds

1950 Compensation, sublimation,
  displacement, projection,
  undoing & conversion:
  the machine
  breaks down.
1951 There was a little boy
  & he had a little eye
  smack in the middle of his forehead.
  When he was wood he was green as Robin Hood,
  but when he was it, he was horrid.
1952 Now that I'm wearing his ring
  Bowwow & Jack Bone
  are quite a proper couple.
  We dote long evenings on his mother.
  I've learned to play canasta.
1953 Now I discover
  looking back at Grimm:
  Rapunzel (rampion)
  is nothing
  but a salad.
1954 "A man could thrive
  pulling weeds. His life
  would not be ill spent
  & best of all
  weeds would survive."

JULY 25

Laughing at Gods

1950 I do not like thee, Dr Freud.
  I don't know why. There is a void,
  neither split pea nor paranoid.
  Beyond trapeze & trapezoid
  I do not find thee, Dr Freud.
1951 Hermes has driven down
  to Brooklyn with his mother
  to find him
  an apartment
  for The Fall.
1952 Bowwow has named
  his kitten Arf-n-Arf.
  "Few things are black
  & white," whispers
  Jack Ambigon.
1953 What appetite
  sent Abraham
  into the witch's garden
  while Sarah
  laughed at God?
1954 The weeder's toil
  does little harm.
  No matter how much
  we hurt, we cannot
  reach the root.

JULY 26

Stepping Stones

1950 Burden brings Freud
  to English so I'm glad
  to have read up on those psychos
  Oedipus & Narcissus.
  All that razz.
1951 I tread
  the secret stepping stones
  that lure us through Poe's "To Helen."
  Nycean, native, naiad, niche,
  & (dim inversion) *hyacinth.*
1952 He's having a week's vacation at The Cape.
  I'm taking care of Arf-n-Arf.
  I brought him home at midnight.
  He went straight
  to his mother's belly & she suckled him.
1953 Pictures talk to Hermes.
  Hermes talks to me.
  I write to Lilian.
  The silence behind
  unframes the mind.
1954 Few things are clear.
  For instance, after many & many a year,
  the game of Peter Pan gets tiresome.
  Wouldn't it be groovy to grow up?
  I don't mean be a Darling or dumb.

JULY 27

Allegory, Epic, Comic Book

1950 Joe has not
  sent his address.
  I hold an apple in one hand,
  paring knife in the other,
  wondering.
1951 I cross the campus.
  Woods. Then garden.
  Then the quad.
  Nature. Romance. Design.
  There's no escaping allegory.
1952 From Lew
  I get epic
  letters: thirty
  pages rolled
  into a little envelope.
1953 Atlantic & Pacific
  toil beneath
  my troubled sleep:
  canned cardboard,
  corrugated corn.
1954 Captain Hook.
  That pirate like a comic book
  is near as many of us ever get
  to ripeness,
  a parent spook not nearly ill-met.

JULY 28

Boxes

1950 Tanner,
  unwitting pander,
  hands on
  an act of contrition
  postmarked Syracuse.
1951 Crossing the same campus
  as a child I'd catch the flagpole
  falling toward me slowly, slow
  as the humming sails
  of my green vertigo.
1952 Lew rambles the boroughs:
  Brooklyn Botanical, Bronx Zoo.
  He apologizes that drunk
  he dashed the pipe I gave him
  off a roof.
1953 I dream of ripping
  boxes. Then I dream
  I'm ripping the same
  boxes. Then I'm
  ripping them again.
1954 Enough!
  There's moonlight stuff
  that really might sustain a crocodile
  ticking down Thames
  toward Nile.

JULY 29

Fathom Five

1950 He comes
  by omnibus
  to meet me in the park,
  the Crescent Park,
  at noon.
1951 In World War II
  the college was a navy training school.
  My crossings rocked upon the swell
  of swarming sailors
  & I knew.
1952 He finds a newsroom open
  at 3:00 AM. He wants a quart
  of beer & a cigar. The Cuban
  calls him behind the counter
  flashing Havana.
1953 My butterfly
  new brawn
  has brains
  of its own.
  I dream of dawn.
1954 I do believe in fairies who are not dull
  as Tinkerbell,
  but pun & pan
  peeling Bermuda:
  Ariel & Caliban.

JULY 30

Jacqueline

1950 We searched the town.
  A crowd of boys
  by Ramsey's Pharmacy
  hailed me:
  "Jacqueline!"
1951 I wove a crow's
  nest of caps
  & bell bottoms,
  weighing anchored buttons
  off each wine-dark hatch.
1952 "Old jokes become
  reality on benders."
  He looks for no epiphany
  more true or hopeful.
  I wonder about Sybil.
1953 I've blown that job.
  Hermes & I take off
  toward Sybil & Lew.
  Lilian will meet our train.
  O little yellow ticket!
1954 Whatever
  I sit down to
  sets me off
  cruising
  Greyhound.

JULY 31

Lobster

1950 "Will you walk
a little faster?"
said the lobster.
My shadow shimmered
at his heel.
1951 A certain red
wildflower floats
on so slim a stem
it seems to hang on air.
I am daily amazed.
1952 He will come down
from his booze pinnacle
all his angels dashed on stone.
I wonder about Sybil
silent & alone.
1953 The river & the train
go south again.
The train lurches & howls.
The river broadens
& deepens.
1954 I miss the Plaza
matinee blowing
my brains out
through a glory
hole. *Gloria!*

AUGUST 1

We Hid in a Thicket

1950 We hid in a thicket.
 Bird song.
 Damp newspapers & broken
 sumac fruit. He sighed:
 I needn't see him to his bus.
1951 Hermes is back
 with the key
 to a room in Brooklyn.
 The desk is oak.
 The bed is Hollywood.
1952 Being
 his bride
 & bird,
 maybe she sings,
 maybe it doesn't matter.
1953 The river drops into the sea.
 We push into Manhattan rather clumsily.
 Lilian, blonde & tall,
 as we crowd round her,
 inhales the city & the shore.
1954 The station john.
 The station johns
 quicken as on
 my knees a freight
 brakes Calvary.

AUGUST 2

What Am I After?

1950 Let's talk about the weather.
I pumped my uncle's bike
clear out of town, clear
down the yellow line of country roads.
Sweatshirt & sunlight.
1951 The imitation Tudor
survives under the El. The elderly
British couple, his hosts,
seem transplanted & vaguely spooky.
So do the roses.
1952 She goes to work.
Walks home.
Maybe he'll be there.
She'll make an evening meal.
Something to warm over while he's gone.
1953 Big girl!
She reigns
handsomer than I remember.
I see what I forgot.
Authority.
1954 Bats infest those trees.
Their shadow mimicry
flits after insects.
What am I
after?

AUGUST 3

After the Flood

1950 The bath of sweat
 washes me out
 of the world:
 salt, oil
 & water.
1951 They're really two
 old ladies he suspects.
 Hermes Poirot
 plots skillfully
 his fall.
1952 Of course he will return.
 Does she know it? Does she doubt?
 Perhaps it is exactly what she knows & doubts.
 She will ask him to forgive her for his faults.
 It's what they're all about.
1953 Lew set up a table on the roof.
 We supped beneath stars,
 the heights & harbor below us.
 Liberty & the Staten ferry.
 Speed of light.
1954 Stranger,
 fee,
 fie,
 foe,
 fumble.

AUGUST 4

Naked Strangers

1950 The yards fill
with neighbors.
Naked strangers spill
spontaneous generations
in the heat.
1951 The world
moves on
to college.
I go back
to high school.
1952 Laura listens
& makes no comment.
Silence walls the enemy.
Mere understanding
cannot scale.
1953 Lilian shone,
a tanned & sun-bleached
long afternoon
on white sand
warming our midnight meal.
1954 I eat
the unborn seed
of the first son.
I devour
the unborn child.

AUGUST 5

Shelters

1950 I build
a little shade
against the sun's
publicity.
I shelter heart & skin.
1951 I try to get in
To Hermes' gladness.
Great expectations
sing us youth away & promise
soaring cities.
1952 Bowwow asks me why
I want to read & buy
so many books. Lying beside him
in the dark motel I say,
"I won't always be young."
1953 Lew read his story about a boy
spelled to an old woman's tales,
their cold hearts beating
together against the summer heat.
It was me & Grandmother Raven.
1954 All I want
is to be
a good boy.
Why must I gorge
on marigold?

AUGUST 6

Gnat & Ghost

1950 Miss Bramble has known me
since I first knew how to read.
She works at County P.
She has introduced me
to a sybil.
1951 Laura will stay.
Sybil & Lew remain.
Nevertheless,
when Hermes goes,
the waves close over me.
1952 He calls me wise
& wants to know how
I've acquired wisdom.
I allow
his flattery.
1953 Hide & seek.
The bodies burn.
So strange to hear & gradually remember
while we huddle round the poet on the cool roof.
Lilian remarks,"Art changes everything."
1954 Sir Harry emerges,
odd bright beetle,
from the host
of gnat & ghost,
my nights & days.

AUGUST 7

I'm Sure It Would Be Wonderful

1950 Sybil comes new to County P.
  She knows a poet.
  She showed me his work
  stuffed into a portable
  liver-colored file.
1951 The novel won't go.
  I tear forty pages
  into tiny pieces
  for the cat's box
  & tend my beans.
1952 He makes it sound
  so woeful to be wise.
  I'm sure it would be wonderful.
  I splutter only
  not dumb.
1953 All evening
  Sybil apologized
  for nothing.
  She hovered just
  herself & very lovely.
1954 We wound a trail
  of sandhills to this wood.
  He spread a blanket under pines.
  He assumed himself
  my lover.

AUGUST 8

My Skin Could Feel the Music

1950 I did not understand a word.
  Still my skin could feel the music.
  I found myself
  the center of the swarming hive
  telling the news.
1951 Poems grow
  from my husbandry.
  I learn it is true:
  the left hand must not know
  but only do.
1952 People pretend at least
  to sympathy for the deformed
  or simply homely.
  I've never heard anyone allow
  the pain of being pretty.
1953 I overflowed.
  Love does
  prevail
  & prosper
  at a meal.
1954 Pine needles
  & mosquitoes sting
  our sweating
  unexpected bodies.
  I tell him who I am.

AUGUST 9

Cold Supper

1950 Someone named Jack Bean
   will bring his poems to
   someone named Sybil who
   will carry them to Albany
   & somebody named Lew.
1951 Jack in the pulpit
   lectures the cat.
   Jack in lady slippers
   minces felicity awhile
   between Sybil & Laura.
1952 American State
   requests that Dad & Moma
   write expressing what
   they hope their son or daughter
   will acquire from a college education.
1953 I stayed three days with Lew & Sybil.
   Met Lilian in Manhattan: *Golden Apple*.
   She took me home. Her parents
   had laid a cold supper for us
   in the livingroom. Fresh linen.
1954 Cynic Sir Harry says
   that shouldn't matter:
   he's married himself.
   Saint Simple sobs.
   "I will be faithful."

Make Our Little Boy a Man

1950 Somebody
in Albany
whose words
wear flesh, run blood
will read my poems.
1951 Lew & Hermes drop
behind to watch me wag.
We stroll down riverside
to see our local artists'
sidewalk show.
1952 They fear to write.
I do it for them. Now I sit
amazed at what I've written.
"We hope the college can
make our little boy a man."
1953 I woke at noon. The hum
of cautious voices in the kitchen
recalled me: here I am
to meet my girlfriend's parents.
They will notice that I tremble.
1954 He remembers
he had such young intentions once.
The car smoulders.
I wish he'd start the motor.
Sir Harry Asphodel.

AUGUST 11

Arm'slength

1950 I typed them clean.
  The folder hung
  at the end of my arm
  like an anchor, like a kite,
  like Laura, like a little brother.
1951 Jack Cat
  behind dark glasses
  reflects.
  At least
  the lenses do.
1952 Do I empathize with Dad & Moma
  or deliver the college
  what it wants to hear?
  Banality tortures
  the poor heart laid bare.
1953 "You tremble, Jack.
  Also you are left-handed.
  How do you propose
  with such flaws
  to provide for our daughter?"
1954 Tomorrow Lilian descends
  with Hermes & Miriam.
  The grail makes its way
  into which this blood
  may spill & be stilled.

AUGUST 12

Promise

1950 We waited together.
  When the bus arrived
  I handed her the poems.
  I glimpsed her seated
  bend to my typescript.
1951 I watch us waft
  & willow over parked enamel:
  Studebaker warps,
  Chrysler promises
  funny house.
1952 What is the world
  that I should want
  to "swim with the current"?
  Roiling kettle
  of old fish.
1953 Mr. & Mrs. Trout
  wanted only to feed me.
  She watches, teases.
  He is a man
  who has lighted.
1954 We hunt
  for an apartment.
  A poor thing
  but charming, we find it
  by late afternoon.

AUGUST 13

Dry Tongue

1950 Ego refracts the imagery of dreams.
  Perhaps the images themselves like stones
  or cuttlefish ripple & cloud the stream.
  Meanwhile what gorgon
  grips my dry tongue?
1951 Paintings leaned
  against the porches, hung on fences,
  outside walls of houses.
  I looked only at trees,
  weeds in the cracked pavements.
1952 At Tanglewood:
  Wagner in the shed,
  Hermes & me & Bowwow on the lawn,
  I notice how white the leaves seem
  in the dark. In the dark.
1953 "Is coming a lobster," called Mr. Trout
  seeing us unhinge ourselves from Henry J,
  back from the beach.
  He was pointing at Hermes.
  We both were burned.
1954 A crooked little landlord
  with a pocketful of keys
  showed us upstairs
  in a little brick house
  on Dove Street.

AUGUST 14

Trying to Put It All Together

1950 "Laura! Waiting
  makes me
  thirsty." Laura
  shrugs expressing
  impatience? Disbelief?
1951 A passing animal pissed
  against derivative
  Monet. "That dog
  is an ironic bitch,"
  laughed Lew lifting his leg.
1952 In the dark.
  Hermes has let me see the painting.
  The back of my head,
  a grace of arm & shoulder.
  Picture of a boy sleeping.
1953 Back home
  I'm trying to put it all together.
  A fabulous depression lights
  folding its black wings
  & stares me down across the room.
1954 It is the queerest nest,
  awkward as a groom.
  Kitchen, livingroom & bath
  open off the hall,
  a separate key for each.

AUGUST 15

Is Anyone Inside?

1950 Sybil called
  to announce:
  I am young
  but I am
  a poet.
1951 I nodded greetings
  passing the house
  where Joe had his apartment.
  Pigeons scattered up
  to Murphy.
1952 Shades
  of faded greens.
  Some of the quiltpatch brightens.
  Hermes maintains
  that green is warm.
1953 Haven't I sloughed
  the old husk?
  What if I haven't?
  What if I have?
  Is anyone inside?
1954 A double bed
  fills an alcove off the livingroom.
  "We'll have the hand-embroidered spread"
  some great grandmother bride
  once made in Germany.

AUGUST 16

Embark for Ithaca

1950 She advised me to read
  Hart Crane. Also the French
  symbolists: Baudelaire,
  Rimbaud & Verlaine.
  "I can pronounce the French."
1951 No one browsed there
  that any of us knew
  to break our circle.
  We wove together.
  We spun the perfect weather.
1952 I neither hope nor fear.
  In three weeks I start college.
  Laura soon embarks for Ithaca.
  Bowwow takes me out or we play cards
  waiting for the old woman to retire.
1953 Why does an insolent
  basilisk sit on my desk
  breathing heavy,
  trying not
  to blink?
1954 The old man fussed & fumbled,
  dumped his keys across the kitchen table.
  We needed four
  including the street door.
  None were labeled.

AUGUST 17

Dry Bread

1950 Quick denotes living.
Jack be quick. I burn,
diminishing candle
in a brass dish
with a little handle.
1951 The local talent:
all derivative.
We condescended,
but I fretted.
"Upon what ground?"
1952 Hermes bought a tuna
sandwich at Tanglewood;
he unwrapped
two slices
of dry bread.
1953 Death by suffocation.
Death by eyes.
Eurydice-Medusa
is the prize
& fatal.
1954 We brought the news
of our dove cote
to Hermes & Miriam.
She is five months
gone as the saying goes.

AUGUST 18

Some Couples

1950 Now I understand
  the trick: jump over
  what you are.
  Jack is the candle.
  The cow is the moon.
1951 "We're all mad here,"
  gravedigger & cat agree.
  Denmark must rot
  & England be queer
  & Jack must go on living in Schenectady.
1952 Ten days I'll have
  in Brooklyn getting to know
  Sybil & Lew: the married couple.
  Ten days I'll have the city & my friends.
  Doesn't the island tremble?
1953 I turn a kind of stone.
  It can really happen.
  Medical records attest
  people can petrify.
  But it is rare & slow.
1954 She doesn't show.
  Why am I eager
  to have her grow?
  She isn't me
  & I am not her baby.

AUGUST 19

Promised Land

1950 Sybil took me
to meet the poet. Lew.
Eternal bus.
I scrubbed myself raw
& put on modesty.
1951 I am the cat.
Am I grave,
digger too?
We sing & grin.
It ain't no sin.
1952 Laura & I
make a farewell.
She will be gone
when I return from Brooklyn.
We will not see each other every day.
1953 Stone crumbles though.
I remember the sorry mummy
at an Albany museum: more
like sand & Laura said,
"I think it's a dirty joke."
1954 Her breasts
have swollen:
wonder!
Beehives
& bibles.

AUGUST 20

Deeps & Shallows

1950 The bus expels us
    (X spells us)
    on Madison at Washington Park.
    Lew lives nearby
    in his fraternity.
1951 The cat sprawls amorous.
    We tease each other in my bed
    until she finds a way
    under the covers
    to my nakedness: her fur.
1952 That space & time should come
    so arbitrary between friends
    seems to me a kind of ignorance
    of nature. Only
    the world's mischance.
1953 The past goes deep.
    I gasp in the shallows.
    Little thing beneath my pillow.
    All my dream
    splits like pea.
1954 Hermes is five months gone.
    I do not mean mourning.
    Like Mary in Luke
    he keeps these things
    & ponders them in his heart.

AUGUST 21

Familiar

1950 He met us at the door.
   The little man.
   What made me think
   the poet would be tall?
   It felt so wrong to tower.
1951 Her nakedness: my fur.
   I've looked up
   familiar:
   a spirit embodied in an animal;
   official of the Inquisition.
1952 We wandered through the town.
   We raided her parents' fridigaire
   at midnight. Things we have done.
   She gave me Hart Crane's *Letters*
   for remembrance.
1953 What have I turned upon?
   I think of Bluejay hanging
   around my old sunflower in the fall.
   His wooing showed me
   I was dry.
1954 We leave them
   in Brooklyn & drive on
   to Long Island & the sun
   where we will take
   our sacerdotal chances.

AUGUST 22

Doting on Little Animals

1950 In the lofty room,
   the poet: swarthy little man,
   his face tending toward farce,
   bad teeth, beautiful
   black hair.
1951 Laura complains
   it's perfectly nasty
   so to dote
   on little animals.
   Was it the cat who farted?
1952 I do not think of Laura coming down.
   Hermes raves & ravishes
   all my attention.
   Lew meets our train
   like some old toy.
1953 Lew writes
   warning me my Lilian's
   a mountain, overbearing mouse.
   "Puddinghead, rethink
   your present thickening."
1954 Days hang like a rosary.
   Saint Simple an Easter Song.
   Childhood re-echoes.
   Everything begins
   with apples & swings.

AUGUST 23

Cat's Whiskers

1950 "Work hard.
  The word
  is your enemy.
  Read William
  Carlos Williams."
1951 Laura shows me
  she can make
  cat's whiskers,
  a trick
  of puckering.
1952 Lew led us
  through tunnels
  & some streets
  to Remsen
  where Sybil waited.
1953 He split hairy wits.
  Mean jumps the moon.
  Basilisk swoons
  & cannot find the energy
  to answer.
1954 Dad & Moma said
  I was a nervous child.
  At school they said,
  "Children are not nervous."
  Lilian says I underestimate the ocean.

AUGUST 24

More Cats

1950 He took my measure
  to brown eyes
  & nodded "Eliot"
  & turned to Sybil.
  They chatted about friends.
1951 She warns me,
  she witches me:
  cat & familiar.
  We clean our claws
  on passing trees.
1952 Ouija
  has grown a cat.
  Competence prowls
  the Brooklyn roofs.
  Wow! Wow!
1953 I don't
  know why
  Lew should
  obstruct
  my passage.
1954 People said
  my laugh
  was funny
  implying
  some wrong.

AUGUST 25

Loitering

1950 He had been arrested
crossing the park.
He was drunk.
He was not. . .
"Loitering," he said.
1951 Laura thinks
her breasts
too big
a different girl
would boast about.
1952 Lew has been sober
two weeks & Sybil seems easy.
He's cooking chicken & rice.
Theresa & Hot Fudge arrive.
Lew doesn't touch the wine.
1953 I write defending
myself, defending
Lilian. Defensive
postures never
look good.
1954 I picked my nose.
I bit my fingernails
& thought I'd never
be a star.
Ugly hands!

AUGUST 26

Kindergarten

1950 Was the euphemy
for Sybil? Her alarm
called for soothing.
He turned it
to laughter.
1951 We pass a bakery
breathing the fresh
warm aroma."Laura,
you should catch yourself
a regular fellow."
1952 Everyone stayed late.
I was not alone
with Sybil & Lew
until morning
breezed in off the roof.
1953 I tell myself
to go to Albany
"& find yourself
the room you've saved
all summer for."
1954 In a kindergarten
playhouse looking out
I didn't laugh,
I didn't cry.
Princess! Princess!

AUGUST 27

Backing Down the Ladder

1950 "I've put my X
   by certain lines
   in which the phrasing thrills
   & is not merely yours.
   I look for more."
1951 We agree to share our lives
   in a platonic marriage.
   I may have lovers,
   so may she.
   We will be true *in our fashion.*
1952 Ouija wakens me
   dropping from the hatch
   onto my bed. Lew follows
   backing down the ladder,
   folded bedding in his arms.
1953 With how little ceremony
   I have detached myself
   from Bowwow, Bluejay,
   Laura. Lilian is all
   my ripeness now.
1954 I watched my playmates
   squeeze themselves from clay.
   Didn't the world die
   five times a day
   when I was five?

AUGUST 28

I Never Learned to Read Music

1950 He looks for better.
He looks for more as fine
but fails to find them.
He looks for me
to make more.

1951 We tell the Pimpernels
we expect we'll marry someday.
We're both surprised to hear us tell.
They're busy over films of Sissysue
on ice.

1952 Breakfast:
Lew tunes in
on morning with
a sweet & fresh
good will.

1953 Summer
regains Paradise,
the devil
selling apples
at the corner.

1954 I never learned
to read music.
A jaundice
kept me home
that month.

AUGUST 29

Dry Toast

1950 I will write wonderful poems for him.
  I will write poems to ravish flesh
  & raze the world. I'll find the words
  will tear the soul out of my body
  & blind his weary eyes.
1951 They plan for Sissysue
  to become a competition
  figure skater. I can't figure
  what their plan has been for Laura.
  Clearly it had to be abandoned.
1952 Sybil & I
  wake passive.
  We can enjoy
  benevolence
  too easily.
1953 Lew
  Lilian.
  Lilian
  Lew.
  What a dry toast to chew.
1954 I learned to talk at the movies.
  In those innocent days
  all the stars
  could articulate
  & used good grammar.

AUGUST 30

Renovations

1950 Renovation has begun
   at County Public:
   carpenters,
   sawdust,
   plaster.
1951 Tomorrow. Friday
   & my friend leaves full
   of hope & fear. This autumnal
   evening we have spent together
   listening to music in his room.
1952 Hermes with girls:
   Theresa wears white
   & Hot Fudge blue.
   They flow like cool springs.
   Bare arms look everything.
1953 Tomorrow I will seek
   a setting for my fall.
   It won't be elegant.
   My little savings
   have to last the year.
1954 I worried about my ignorance.
   Everybody shared
   some terrible
   important secret
   they kept from me.

AUGUST 31

Evensong

1950 One little carpenter
whistles while he works.
But it's all one note
& a boon when he begins to saw.
Even the hammers sing.
1951 "Four years ago
I was thirteen. Already
at my *bar mitzvah* I said,
TODAY I AM A MAN.
Tonight I am a boy."
1952 I follow down the afternoons
with Hermes & Theresa & Hot Fudge.
Lew writes poems.
He reads to us at meals
most evenings.
1953 I have taken
a very nice room
at the Hudson Arms.
For nine dollars a week
I may throw myself into the river.
1954 I was always unbuttoned.
I had to wear suspenders.
Tomorrow I get married
in my belt
& zipper fly.

SEPTEMBER 1

Plaster Ascends

1950 A sawdust
   din shivers
   each neat
   BE QUIET.
   Plaster ascends.
1951 Labor Day
   toils summer
   toward an end.
   Laura & Sybil, Lew & Jack
   take a picnic to Saint Panther.
1952 After *Pal Joey* a pigeon
   shits on my shoulder crossing
   Shuberts Alley. We were all
   crossing Shuberts Alley:
   the pigeon, my shoulder & I.
1953 Rain falls outside my window,
   a known monotony.
   The choice resides:
   Lew or Lilian.
   Sybil won't intercede.
1954 Hermes & Miriam by train.
   Moma & Dad by car.
   The wedding chimes one.
   Small church: clapboard.
   The usual pigeons.

SEPTEMBER 2

Caprice

1950 Early morning fog
teases my progress.
Dinosaurs & dickens
prowl the little distance.
As I approach, fog retreats.
1951 Laura fed me my first shrimp.
She brings shrimp to our feast.
I can't blame Hermes
for rushing early
to his new. . .
1952 I can never persuade Lew
of the elegance of dangled
modifiers carefully misplaced
like certain people fate
capriciously assigns.
1953 Dismentored
I'll survive.
Lew demands I choose.
I have no choice.
Expel each weeping angel.
1954 I wade mid-morning
in the wake of our wedding night
on errands I half forget.
The new man wants only one rose
to take home to his new woman.

SEPTEMBER 3

The Poets Hover

1950 All the poets
  Lew & Sybil named
  hover at my fingertips.
  Their weight transports me.
  My desk floats.
1951 Lew fed me my first tongue.
  We have tongue sandwiches.
  They don't say much.
  The deviled eggs
  seduce me.
1952 The best caprice is an ineptness apt.
  I'm back. A college student at long last.
  Snatches of *Pal Joey* & *New Faces* on the bus.
  They hand me a schedule. One elective:
  Introduction to Philosophy.
1953 "A word is no
  light matter,"
  writes Edith Hamilton.
  Clearly it is
  no matter.
1954 I am not Narcissus.
  I have become
  his reflection in the pond.
  How can the world not know
  that we have drowned?

SEPTEMBER 4

Fate Is Not Serious

1950 Poor Baudelaire!
  The military father,
  commercial world,
  respectability.
  Fate is not serious.
1951 Tomorrow I go back
  to high school.
  Bound. Unbound.
  I have a future
  & I'll do.
1952 I watch my fellow frosh
  torment some swishing Charlie
  & I'm grateful
  that at seventeen
  I learned to walk.
1953 We met a train today.
  Hermes & I welcomed Mr. Bear
  from Pennsylvania, seven feet
  of Hermes' classmate
  arriving for a weekend.
1954 After our third night
  Lilian suffered a terrible
  flow of blood. The doctor
  says it's not unusual
  after first intercourse.

SEPTEMBER 5

Seducing Respectable Verlaine

1950 Rimbaud,
   the terrible child,
   seduces respectable Verlaine.
   We do what we can
   to insure our season in hell.
1951 I've had no lover
   since Joe. Lew's kiss,
   my trumpery crush on Welkin.
   That's all.
   I've not been vagrant.
1952 New freshmen are tested.
   They probe our psyches
   with five hundred statements.
   True or False: "I suffer
   diarrhea daily."
1953 Mr. Bear
   is lots of meat.
   His sad eyes
   make me forget
   my woe.
1954 Jack in the Box
   & Lady Slipper
   kick through leaves,
   scuff home
   from super market.

SEPTEMBER 6

Wayside Weeds

1950 He plots
  "a divine
  disordering
  of all the senses."
  We plot.
1951 "Welkin
  doesn't work here
  anymore."
  The sky is fallen,
  left no forwarding.
1952 "Nobody understands me."
  I make it *true*
  knowing the markers
  won't appreciate
  my glee.
1953 I wonder
  Hermes
  let us out alone.
  Wayward embraces
  in the wayside weeds.
1954 "Order is a lovely
  thing. On disarray
  it lays its wing
  teaching simplicity
  to sing."

SEPTEMBER 7

Homework

1950 Running away
  to join the revolution
  he is raped
  by his fellow soldiers.
  Goes home. But not to stay.
1951 A mood
  of simple discipline
  prevails.
  I do my homework,
  love my friends.
1952 The present barrage
  cannot distract
  my heart which dwells
  in Brooklyn: Hermes
  & Hot Fudge.
1953 I say goodbye
  to Hermes & Mr. Bear.
  "We'll meet again. . ."
  I'm at the dorm
  to welcome Lilian.
1954 Hermes & Miriam
  bring zinnias
  & pictures of our wedding.
  On the table
  milk & honey.

SEPTEMBER 8

Repenting Again & Again

1950 Verlaine repents,
   repents again.
   I know this man
   who paws his boys & beads
   at target practice.
1951 I play the phonograph
   in my closed room:
   Wagner, Stravinsky.
   Swan Lake & Les Sylphides.
   I meditate in fifth position.
1952 At a bar
   I flirted
   with a stranger
   & invited him
   into our company.
1953 My newest poem embraces
   the infernal embrace
   of Paolo & Francesca.
   Paolo was her penance.
   The husband was her sin.
1954 The wedding pictures:
   I look a perfect man
   of business in my blue;
   Lilian resembles
   her mother.

SEPTEMBER 9

Music Is My Only Appetite

1950 He could not murder
either himself or the boy.
He could not satisfy
either a wife or a lover.
But he could write poems.
1951 Music is my only appetite.
My body stands quite still.
I close my eyes.
My ears eat harmonies.
My spirit dances.
1952 Hermes took me aside
next morning to scold.
He loves me & my promiscuity
hurts. I do not understand.
What has sex got to do with us?
1953 Ugliness prevails
in this world & hell.
I do not care
that Pandemonium is all
& hell is where I am.
1954 Moma brings news:
Tom Cat is dead.
He came home one morning,
complained about his breakfast,
napped. Then wouldn't wake.

SEPTEMBER 10

Tin Man

1950 How reluctantly I sleep!
I turn from book to book
returning to *Season in Hell*.
Cries of agony were heard welling
from the shed where he wrote these words.
1951 Dick doesn't count.
Latin, Plane
Geometry,
Biology,
& bed.
1952 We trod our troubles
roaming the borough streets
witnessing arrests, men
walking their boxers,
sunrise on Manhattan Bridge.
1953 "I could stay young and chipper
and I'd lock it with a zipper
if I only had a heart."
Albany harbors me,
but not the Hudson Arms.
1954 She made my father bury him.
"So the garbage men didn't get him."
When the collectors came he ran
to hide in the dirty laundry
where he was born.

SEPTEMBER 11

We Had to Keep Him Tied up in the Yard

1950 He ran away
 the last time
 to sell guns
 to a thousand
 African Verlaines.
1951 Hermes' first letter
 bloats on much news
 from his new world.
 What shall I write?
 I have only my new repose.
1952 A derelict shuffled toward us
 begging a nickle.
 We emptied our pockets
 to give him every nickle
 we could find.
1953 Even as I arrived
 they raised the rent.
 I could barely pay nine.
 My dad stood smoking beside his gaping trunk.
 "Farewell, Hudson Arms."
1954 Moma is a mistress of epitaph:
 "She was my friend."
 "The garbage men didn't get him."
 She'll say of my dead body in the ground,
 "We had to keep him tied up in the yard."

SEPTEMBER 12

House & Garden

1950 *Illuminations.*
Drunken Boat.
Les Fleurs du Mal.
"Tu le connais, Lecteur."
I know what I have to do.
1951 "All my events,
Dear Friend,
occur inside.
Otherwise, nothing happens.
I'm fiercely at home.
1952 The meanest hour
wolfs our straw
house down.
Timon of Manhattan
adores the obvious.
1953 Dad drove me around.
We found a drab room
in an ugly flat
on North Lake, the landlord
a Pinkerton detective.
1954 "Garden,"
my new poem,
allows the moon
to break through trees
& make the roses bleed.

SEPTEMBER 13

Cocktails

1950 They call me out of work
to join them at a bar.
Lew orders me cocktails.
I have five. They put me
in a taxi after closing.
1951 Life drifts as if it ought.
I study, read & write.
Laura picks me up from work.
Our walk is slow,
our conversation bright.
1952 My last night in Brooklyn.
Hot Fudge stayed.
We slept on the roof.
She would have taken me.
I was afraid.
1953 I moved
right in.
Shouldn't Jack
share squalor
with a dick?
1954 Tiger brings
a purple plant
from Paraguay.
The frau enacts
dismay.

SEPTEMBER 14

I'm Here

1950 In Moma's bathroom
I threw up.
The kitchen & bedroom
flew round
like trapped birds.
1951 The restless boy
I've known
since I was nine
reminds me:
insomnia.
1952 I learn new names.
I'm almost sure
Minerva won't fall on me.
She's only plaster
& I'm here.
1953 He showed me
his badge
upon request.
He didn't detect
I was flirting.
1954 He glanced back
halfway up the block.
I saw him from the window
shake the dust
off his feet.

SEPTEMBER 15

Feeling Left-Handed

1950 We move
  toward unmoved
  perfection.
  Death
  is God.
1951 I dreamed
  a thief broke
  through my bedroom window,
  a gnome who stole
  the fourth wall.
1952 Bowwow & I were invited to a party.
  We had met a Mr. Random at Lollipop's
  who had in tow a Caravaggio.
  I always feel left-handed
  in such company.
1953 I've turned the room
  into a small Van Gogh.
  New-painted walls
  look about to fall
  into the sea.
1954 Lew scythes
  through my "Garden."
  I'm *facile* & he lays
  it all on Lilian.
  I thought he had more logic.

SEPTEMBER 16

Strange Shift

1950 Joe rented a car
  & drove to a deserted beach.
  Trying to find reverse
  on the strange shift,
  he nearly dumped us in the lake.
1951 The little man
  waddled away
  lugging the big wall,
  one of Alice's
  courtroom pack.
1952 Mr. Random departing
  said he would invite us to a party.
  Lollipop advised we shouldn't hold our breath.
  The invitation came by phone
  to Bowwow the following morning.
1953 I made a mistake
  showing Lew's letter to Lilian.
  She is scarcely reassured
  that I have chosen.
  I should have made up some story.
1954 I write a letter.
  Lew & Sybil
  gutter & go out.
  I turn to *Saint Simple.*
  I think about odes.

SEPTEMBER 17

Spotlighted in the Darkened Room

1950 God
  doesn't taste
  as I remember,
  neither bread
  nor wine.
1951 I can't imagine
  a more pointless dream.
  Might not the thief
  have been Orpheus
  blowing a trumpet?
1952 Caravaggio was absent.
  Our host took care
  to seat me in a velvet chair.
  Spotlighted in the darkened room,
  I made the point of the party.
1953 Our major production
  this fall
  is *Trojan Women*.
  I have been cast
  as Talthybius.
1954 Birth
  & Circumcision.
  Baptism.
  Temptations
  & Stations.

SEPTEMBER 18

Sacraments

1950 What can
one sing
for the fall?
when bittersweet
is all.
1951 In Biology I learn
the signs of life are digestion,
growth, respiration, excretion,
motion, reproduction, irritability.
It does not seem enough.
1952 He showed me
to the bathroom.
Then he locked us in
together.
I tried to pee.
1953 Lilian
will lead
the chorus.
Meanwhile Herr Brain
directs Marlowe's *Faustus*.
1954 *Saint Simple*
An Easter Song.
The Christian
sacraments.
My life.

SEPTEMBER 19

The Life of Christ

1950 I sit with Lew & Sybil
   on Friday nights in bars.
   I'm learning how to drink
   while I tell them what I think
   Hart Crane's about.
1951 Irritability
   is reflex.
   Reflection
   is something else.
   Life exceeds nature.
1952 It took me half an hour
   to convince him he had guests.
   That I had come with Bowwow
   & was determined
   to go home with him.
1953 Ross of the organic voice
   elocutes Faustus
   to everyone's satisfaction.
   I think he's boring
   as a gong.
1954 The life
   of Christ
   attended by
   Tiger, Lily,
   Saint Simple & Tigerlily.

SEPTEMBER 20

The Point of the Story

1950 I'm willing to understand the poet.
His strange words
mean what they say.
I must allow my ears
to instruct my brain.
1951 After biology,
after history, psychology,
after all the textbooks,
Laura, for instance,
remains.
1952 The point of the story
is simply that I fought off Mr. Random.
But Bowwow
does not
believe me.
1953 Rehearsals
every night.
From Troy I return
to *Beowulf* & roaches.
Herr Brain knocks.
1954 Tiger prowls:
maleness.
Lily embraces:
shepherdess.
Romance.

SEPTEMBER 21

The Brain Has Its Reasons

1950 Now that
the idea
of deluge
has withdrawn,
I'm dry.
1951 Poets
who are
not fools
write
for themselves.
1952 He weeps
& calls me a whore.
The Studebaker throbs.
"Be reasonable.
Blow your nose."
1953 Herr Brain dislikes
everybody
with good reason.
The brain
has its reasons.
1954 Participation
in an earthly life.
Saint Simple
remakes the male.
He takes a wife.

SEPTEMBER 22

The Dark House of the Priests

1950 I grew up
in the parish of St Columba.
Behind the clapboard church
the dark house of the priests
stood shaded under elms.
1951 Sometimes I understand
Lew's impatience with Sybil.
Laura hangs on me
with such awe
my heart withers.
1952 In a pique I tell him,
"After Lollipop's party last summer
while you were drunk
& kissing me goodnight your best friend Buff
had his fist in my pants & brought me off."
1953 He wants me
to be gay
as if it were
something
numinous.
1954 Tigerlily:
resurrection.
God
flowers
out of death.

SEPTEMBER 23

Green Street

1950 Whenever I passed
  I felt something unspeakable
  had happened to me
  in that rectory.
  Still I can't remember.
1951 I write to Hermes. "Good
  friend Andre Gide
  spins his new grave
  singing, "Nothing
  is unnatural."
1952 Now he wants to treat me
  to a hotel weekend in Albany.
  It would be an improvement
  on parking & his mother
  & waiting in line at Mash's.
1953 We are noctambulous.
  After I have taken Lilian home,
  we roam from bar to bar
  or all-night diner.
  I picked a kitten up on Green Street.
1954 Procession struts
  the simple sentence.
  After names & attributes
  verbs lift us
  toward objects.

SEPTEMBER 24

Maybe I was Aborted

1950 Maybe I was baptized there.
I was circumcized in hospital
when I was nine.
So it wasn't that.
Maybe I was aborted.
1951 People tempt me.
"Come out of the garden."
I give them the top of my mind.
I will not be plucked
to wither & die in the sun.
1952 A girl as large as she is loud
accosted me today as we
were gathering for French.
"O Gide!" she effused.
I was carrying *Autumn Leaves.*
1953 I'm calling the rescued kitten
Hecuba in recognition of our play
& her fallen state.
The landlord & his dog
have no objections.
1954 Lew hasn't answered.
His silence
bloats expectation.
Tiger stays away.
He will. He will.

SEPTEMBER 25

Tales of Hoffman

1950 The things we do
  to children & call it
  school. Small wonder
  we can't grow up nice
  like other animals.
1951 *Tales of Hoffman.*
  Robert Helpman.
  Why is my world
  tan gabardine
  & scrubbed faces?
1952 I begin to know people
  at the college. Dixie
  reminds me of Hot Fudge.
  A senior named Tubbs
  asked me to try out for a play.
1953 The dog is too old to care.
  The landlord is rarely at home.
  He is working under cover
  at a mushroom factory.
  I can't fathom why.
1954 I take the garbage down.
  I do that rather well.
  I'm also very good
  at scrubbing floors
  & toilet bowls.

SEPTEMBER 26

Numbers

1950 We long divided every day.
   I put down numbers.
   Numbers tumbled from my brain.
   Nothing has ever bored me more
   than long division.
1951 Robert Helpman draws
   a cautionary finger across his lips.
   Pamela Brown (as Hermes)
   sustains her friend
   in his illusion.
1952 Jesse has graduated.
   People look odd
   when I use his name
   so I've stopped.
   Meanwhile I have been cast.
1953 I come home on Saturdays
   to fetch my week's allowance
   & a little sleep.
   Moma provides a bag of groceries.
   Dad drives me back on Sunday mornings.
1954 This evening I composed
   the compound subject
   of the first sentence
   of *Saint Simple.*"Fish
   prepare for saints."

SEPTEMBER 27

Less Than Shadow

1950 That was fifth grade.
  They said I couldn't read.
  They had my foreskin.
  I believed I was dumb & wondered
  when they would take the rest.
1951 Hoffman
  in the end
  sits drunk,
  abandoned, lone
  & less than shadow.
1952 The other actors,
  veteran seniors,
  practice outrage. Then,
  on stage, all affectations
  thaw, melt, drift away.
1953 Sunday evenings
  belong to Lilian.
  We study together,
  have a few beers,
  go to a movie.
1954 The summer child
  foreshadows
  "slow time,"
  a flower
  gathering flowers.

SEPTEMBER 28

Best Courses

1950 I planned
   to be a woman
   so it didn't matter
   what they did to me
   or made me do.
1951 Lew warns me off
   Hoffman:
   precious, affected
   & the worst
   of influences.
1952 *How He Lied to her Husband*
   is George Bernard Shaw's
   preliminary sketch for *Candida*.
   Of course
   I am the poet.
1953 I'm writing poems
   for Christmas presents.
   Haiku for Hot Fudge:
   the cat in twenty poses.
   Muff is a must.
1954 My best course
   is Milton with Dr. Fran.
   In fifty words
   she can suggest
   that we open a window.

SEPTEMBER 29

L'Allegro

1950 I sang,
  I danced
  in Moma's clothes.
  Childhood
  bled slow.
1951 A train
  will take me
  to Hermes & Manhattan.
  He will show me
  THE CITY.
1952 Tubbs, soft & fat
  behind his cigarette,
  teaches me how to breathe.
  College is wonderful.
  I'll soon know everything.
1953 I found a used condom
  in the kitchen trash.
  The dick has been home.
  He won't detect
  where I spent the night.
1954 The Lady of *Comus*
  & Cambridge says
  the poet
  must become
  the perfect poem.

SEPTEMBER 30

Yellow

1950 A classmate
saw me with Lew & Sybil.
"Who are those people?
That's not what I've heard
about that man."
1951 After midnight.
What can I say?
Judy Garland
at the Palace
Two a Day.
1952 Timid Bluejay,
a sophomore,
holds book.
Asks if he may
walk me to my bus.
1953 When I want a bath
I have to explode a match
inside a tank with gas.
The water runs yellow
into the tub.
1954 Milton makes cleanliness
the still point
of his vocation.
Rimbaud wrote,
"I filthify myself."

OCTOBER 1

I Agree with Heracleitus

1950 His deciduous head
   on a platter,
   a turd
   under a bush.
   Indistinguishable!
1951 Perched
   on the apron,
   dirty face,
   she's bum's rush
   "Over the Rainbow."
1952 We've barely met.
   He's telling me
   I am his soul
   he's been seeking
   for twenty years.
1953 Hecuba sleeps in my hair.
   She thinks peroxide
   is her mother.
   I cannot induce her
   to use her box.
1954 The road from Thebes to Athens
   is not the road from Athens to Thebes,
   but I agree with Heracleitus:
   the way up & the way down
   are one way.

OCTOBER 2

Spilled Beans

1950 I spill my *Beans*
   to Hermes. His room
   swarms in a sweat.
   He pants to meet
   poet & prophetess.
1951 We rode the Staten Island ferry
   shouting Millay across the waters.
   The skyline emerged from fog.
   Small rain swept the waves.
   Hermes! The city & the sea.
1952 I've read Plato.
   Still I let
   one bus go by
   & listen for another
   twenty minutes.
1953 Herr Brain wooed me
   through the afternoon.
   I arrived drunk
   & late for rehearsal.
   Professor Pet already doesn't like me.
1954 Saint Simple
   counts his words.
   Five hundred
   make a paragraph.
   Jack Carpenter.

OCTOBER 3

Buying Olympia

1950 Welkin teaches Senior English,
also Journalism to the Juniors.
Laura & I both have him.
Such a mustache!
Squirrel Nutkin.
1951 Now I have been to the city
its hundred voices haunt
my skin. Its after image
blurs my vision.
I'm Hoffman buying Olympia.
1952 What traffic has such jade
as I with bluejays?
I had better
mind my bus
& business.
1953 Professor Pet directs me
away from my intentions.
I'd have made Talthybius
unnerved by women's woe.
He makes me a ruffian.
1954 I am Ross in Pet's *Macbeth*.
I bring bad news to Lady Macduff.
Ours is the bittersweet moment
upon which hell is broken
& breaks loose.

OCTOBER 4

He Dances

1950 He sucks a pipe
  through classes,
  reeks tobacco.
  I suspect
  a Bourbon undertow.
1951 Hermes,
  the city
  dances.
  Why
  shouldn't I?
1952 Bluejay wants
  to build a nest.
  I'm broken sticks
  & scattered straw.
  He'd put me together.
1953 At first
  I hated & resisted
  his gangster Greek,
  the strut & muscle
  show of strength.
1954 Lilian makes sure
  I have always
  money in my pocket.
  We have beer with lunch,
  wine with every dinner.

OCTOBER 5

The Husband Rises Bloated from the Tub

1950 He reads us e e cummings,
Gertrude Stein, & tells us
about William James'
spiritualism & experiments
with automatic writing.
1951 Chance & determinisms
govern ordinary people
who are content to fit
unamazed in a maze.
I forge a destiny.
1952 Here I am
with Bowwow
in a big hotel
looking downhill
toward the river.
1953 But it is fun
surprising everyone
(including me):
what a butcher
I can be!
1954 We see *Diabolique*. I nearly die
when the husband rises bloated from the tub.
Lilian is bored & can't imagine why
I'm thrilled. Yet this same woman screams
if I come quietly into the room.

OCTOBER 6

A Gnome Approaches

1950 Coincidence evokes.
   While Welkin urges us to pull
   our psyches through our pens,
   a gnome approaches me at County P
   asking where we keep the occult.
1951 Nothing happens to me
   that my spirit hasn't planned.
   Her name is Mum,
   extraordinary flower
   blossoming *deja vu*.
1952 "Shine on,
   harvest moon."
   You're off
   your rocker,
   out of tune.
1953 Hermes & Mr. Bear
   will come to see our play.
   Hermes will sleep on the sofa.
   Mr. Bear will sleep with me.
   I buy Kentucky.
1954 "You were unexpected."
   How can that be?
   The dream
   come true
   can kill.

OCTOBER 7

Strangers

1950 This library gnome reminded me of Pandora.
Creepy strangers often do
although Pandora
neither crept
nor estranged.
1951 The world insists it's real.
I'm enjoying *The Grass Harp*.
Lew laughs
at my poor taste
& the world's pretension.
1952 At last I have a footing:
college, new people,
a part in a play,
a future.
My poor heart daily oozes suicide.
1953 Herr Brain organized a Cocteau festival:
Blood of a Poet, Queen's Lover, Strange Ones.
The incestuous sister announces:
"We must make life so complicated
it becomes impossible."
1954 I write the compound subject
of the first sentence
of *Saint Simple*.
I write it again.
Again & again.

OCTOBER 8

Cosmos & Psyche

1950 I did
   think it odd
   how he got fatter
   every time my glance
   chanced upon him.
1951 Nature abhors
   the vacuum it is.
   Cosmos & psyche.
   Such an enormous
   vacancy!
1952 I play
   my Grampa Bean's
   straight razor
   across my wrists
   like fiddlesticks.
1953 My life is not
   impossible because
   I have no substance,
   have no conscience,
   no dimension.
1954 They merrily
   carry the cross.
   My trouble is
   I can't get
   to the verb.

OCTOBER 9

Basin Street

1950 "Do you believe?" asked the gnome.
   I said I didn't know.
   Of course I do
   believe in ghosts.
   They're me & you.
1951 Nothing to go on.
   My dream of Laura.
   Sybil & Lew.
   Creation *ex nihilo*.
   Hermes perhaps is real.
1952 What's St. Louis to my blues?
   "Mood Indigo"
   was the theme
   of Joe's night show.
   Where's Basin Street?
1953 I fall in love again:
   "Always wanted to."
   What does it mean?
   Be sure the vaseline
   is tucked behind your pillow.
1954 We had too much wine
   & never got our dinner.
   After love-making Lilian
   fell asleep & I went out
   looking for Dick.

OCTOBER 10

What Needs Singing

1950 I didn't tell him
  my bad news. Clearly
  he needs old spooks
  to tell his prayers to.
  "Give us this day."
1951 How can I hope?
  I do not know
  what is strong
  or what is beautiful
  or what needs singing.
1952 Love's old
  sweet song.
  Jack, scrub
  your head clean
  of cheap music.
1953 I know my lines
  & business so well
  they go without thinking.
  A precise puppet nightly
  orders Astyanax murdered.
1954 Dick or Peter.
  Marty called his
  John Thomas.
  What does it matter
  what you call it?

OCTOBER 11

Crowing

1950 Miss Shrimp & I
  move to laughter,
  unpredictable issue
  through cumulus:
  sunlight or lightning?
1951 Lew has stormed out on us again.
  He never sees
  her fine indifference.
  She misgives herself in orbit
  like the moon.
1952 I am dumb
  to brood despondent.
  Bowwow passifies my body,
  Bluejay courts my soul,
  & the play's the thing.
1953 Chorus rehearsals
  were tedious. Now
  the several women
  have become
  one voice.
1954 Any cocky
  dude'll do
  to bring me to
  my knees
  at the sunrise altar.

OCTOBER 12

Islands

1950 Lew maintains promiscuity
"comes natural." Sybil admires
my powers of observation.
I can see that Lew
rarely practices his premise.
1951 Laura has spunk
to sass the world & me.
She will not weep
for love. I fancy her
throwing the last stone.
1952 Bluejay wants a coy mistress.
I will allow him
to be slow
counting the steps of the sun
toward wherever he wishes to go.
1953 The weave
of voices
naming gods
& islands
elates our woe.
1954 Men in the street
are tomb or tabernacle.
Rend the veil.
Sunder the stone.
Lazarus, come.

OCTOBER 13

Graveyard Ditties

1950 Sybil has come full time to County P
    & taken an apartment in town.
    I walk her home.
    We cut through Saint Panther.
    The golden fall.
1951 One Sunday afternoon
    when I was barely twelve
    I held my breath
    beneath my parents' bed
    while they made love.
1952 He presses
    into my daisy hand
    Shakespeare's
    Sonnet 109
    on onion skin.
1953 *Faustus* has come off.
    A shadowshow.
    Chiaroscuro
    carved the players
    into Caligari forms.
1954 Life is a blow.
    It comes hard
    to know
    I am the hammer
    & the nail.

OCTOBER 14

A Little Plastic Casket

1950 Lew's moving in.
  He's broke & hasn't
  anywhere to go.
  Catlike the couple circle
  on the worn linoleum.
1951 I had been home alone
  putting on Moma's dresses.
  I was in their room
  when I heard them
  in the hall & hid.
1952 Grease paint:
  black opera cape
  lined with scarlet:
  dress rehearsal:
  nearly real.
1953 Everynight I take Astyanax
  off stage & bring him back
  a corpse on his father's shield.
  Troy burns
  & I walk Lilian to her dorm.
1954 Lilian takes exquisite
  care of her diaphragm.
  Washed & powdered
  it gets laid away
  in a little plastic casket.

OCTOBER 15

"Love Virtue / She Alone is Free"

1950 Our walks glimmer,
  shimmer indifferent
  to the passing world.
  She makes me see
  the silences in trees.
1951 They had gone
  to *The Lost Weekend*
  & returned early.
  I listened to him
  tease her into bed.
1952 That fat girl
  in my French class
  appeared backstage
  to say she admired my performance
  & I couldn't remember her name.
1953 Near dawn
  I found I'd lost my key.
  Herr Brain
  invited me
  to share his bed.
1954 Asked to read
  the epilogue from *Comus*
  aloud in class,
  I saw that words
  can walk on water.

OCTOBER 16

Stepping Toward Sunday

1950 Joe came to town
   & called me
   at County P.
   We just don't make it
   without Murphy.
1951 I kept very quiet.
   As I stepped
   into my Sunday slacks
   I saw my father's semen
   on the spread.
1952 "Lilian," hissed Tubbs. I tried
   to be pleasant to her at the cast party.
   Someone named Brain
   got in everybody's way.
   Bluejay absented from felicity.
1953 Brain burned beside me.
   His high-school
   English teacher
   was found one morning
   hanging in the boys' shower.
1954 They carry
   & they care.
   I reach
   the essential verbs.
   But all seems shallow now.

OCTOBER 17

The Flood Enspells

1950 Automatic writing.
  I must keep
  a second journal:
  Logic of the Soul.
  The flood enspells me.
1951 A splash of pearl
  on the white hobnail.
  Silk on my fingertip,
  very ripe pear
  on my tongue.
1952 Dixie made an entrance
  in a man's suit, shirt & tie,
  sensible Oxfords, flicking
  her ashes in everybody's beer.
  My mug ran over.
1953 Herr Brain atones.
  I blew him
  to kingdom come
  or sunrise
  as it's called by some.
1954 Find courage.
  Saint Simple
  tells true.
  It is I
  who lie.

OCTOBER 18

First Hand

1950 *Logic
of the Soul*
overweens.
I'll call it
First Hand.
1951 What did I think or feel?
That I mustn't get caught.
I haven't worn women's
clothes again.
Except one Hallowe'en.
1952 Dame Agnes,
who chairs
the Department
of Drama,
embraced me.
1953 I tell Brain:
enact folly,
follow folly's flag.
Otherwise,
nothing comes.
1954 It isn't
necessary to hide
this little book.
Lilian won't look.
She did that once.

OCTOBER 19

In the Dark

1950 "The blackamoor blows back
    the colored lights.
    Dancers illuminate
    & cherry tree evolves
    spindrift against the night."
1951 Letters from Hermes
    brighten my suspense.
    There is a world: A CITY.
    He sketches a signature:
    eyeglasses & a nose.
1952 I decide on the bus
    the silly thing to do.
    I'm going to love Bluejay
    because he is a mess
    & it will hurt.
1953 Be a fool.
    You can't be otherwise.
    The consequences never match the choice
    & irony is always learned too late.
    The masks that frown & grin are one.
1954 I shared my *Beans*
    with Hermes & Laura.
    Since then
    I've sown them in the dark.
    I'm learning what people want.

OCTOBER 20

The Chanted Mass

1950 "Paper kites swarm welkin
teasing the sun. My anemones
walk on water.
Rain drops the queen
to the rump of the sea."
1951 This Latin of the schools,
Caesar & Cicero & Virgil,
is quite another language
from the chanted mass
of childhood.
1952 Our daily lunch & coffee party
greens a corner of the cafeteria:
Dixie, Herr Brain & Tubbs.
Lilian joined us today.
Bluejay shies away.
1953 I'll use my brain
until big Mr. Bear
with a hug
like a rug
warms my grey matter.
1954 Dad & Moma
tried so hard
to teach me.
Do what you will
but don't tell.

OCTOBER 21

The Unsignifying Music

1950 It's not so easy
to let go of words.
They want to be things.
Image & atom fuse
& sometimes fizzle.
1951 Different as *hick* from *hush*.
I prefer the dark lushness
that rushes my ears, the past
welling like blood up my head,
the unsignifying music.
1952 Bluejay intercepts me
on my way from class,
woos me away
to the park
where we can be alone.
1953 In dress rehearsal now,
trying to concentrate,
taming an alien
costume. Hang
the lights!
1954 Put everything aside.
Think about odes.
Iambic pentameter
like Spenser's
ideal knights.

OCTOBER 22

Skylark

1950 Tripping the clown
   Lew says Welkin
   sounds an inspired
   teacher. "Lecher?"
   He winks me down.
1951 Little Jack couldn't get enough
   of church & the movies.
   Incense & popcorn
   filled the dark
   confessional.
1952 There he can sing
   premeditated song,
   romantic claptrap.
   The bluejay squawks,
   noisy bird.
1953 Someone sets up a ladder
   exactly where I stand
   to stare the women down.
   I am blinded by follow spots
   as Cassandra dances.
1954 What is eleven lines that rhyme?
   AA * B * A * BB * C * A * C * DD:
   establish, venture & return, arrive.
   Begin again, recall. Then close.
   A STANZA.

OCTOBER 23

Bas Relief

1950 Lew names my enthusiasm
   schoolboy crush.
   "On Welkin?"
   A welcome relief
   after Burden & old maids.
1951 *Via dolorosa,*
   oleum sanctorum,
   stabat mater,
   pange, lingua,
   missa et confiteor.
1952 I know
   the formula & moment
   to silence his chatter.
   I offer him my challenge.
   "I love you."
1953 Silent above the chorus,
   smudgepots smoking Troy,
   stinging my eyes & nostrils,
   I end up on the wall.
   The broken male.
1954 The movement,
   formal & ideal,
   of the stanza
   stands behind
   the feeling cadence.

OCTOBER 24

To Multiply the Light

1950 I read.
  I study
  The Bridge,
  The Wasteland,
  A Season in Hell.
1951 I didn't understand a word of it.
  The words sang like the candles.
  I crossed my eyes to multiply
  the light. I wished
  I could cross my ears.
1952 Now that
  he's won
  the rose
  what's he
  gonna do?
1953 Yesterday
  came Hermes
  with Mr. Bear:
  Polaris! O!
  Opening night.
1954 *Walking in Snow: to Gertrude Stein: an Ode:*
  "How can we know it is snowing how can we know?"
  Every morning after Lilian
  has left for class
  I listen to *Four Saints.*

OCTOBER 25

Counterfeiters

1950 Lew praised
Andre Gide's
The Counterfeiters.
I'm reading Andre Gide's
The Counterfeiters.
1951 It is a shame
to learn words mean,
to learn what the words mean,
to learn that words are mean.
The words. The word.
1952 He takes me to his dormitory
knowing his roommate will be out.
He strips me solemnly,
his hands swarming my body
like a potter forming Adam.
1953 Can we be
deceiving anyone?
Hermes must guess
what's going on.
He's making it so easy.
1954 I leave early
for rehearsals
so I can cruise
the park. Life
lags unimportant.

OCTOBER 26

Orphics

1950 *The Immoralist.*
Pastoral Symphony.
Straight is the Gate.
The Journals.
If It Die.
1951 I wanted music
& resisted meaning.
Moma got worried
when I wouldn't talk
till I was four.
1952 He rakes my body
like a Japanese gardener
sculpturing sand.
"Bluejay,
the cat!"
1953 I flirt
with Mr. Bear
at dinner.
Hermes & Lilian
won't look.
1954 "Poor Yorick!"
I know him.
He's no one
but Fat Jack
come back to haunt the poet.

OCTOBER 27

Words & the World

1950 I want only
  to be a god
  among my gods.
  The ravaged company.
  We are the words.
1951 All I recall
  of the world
  before I learned
  the words
  is dust & sunlight.
1952 I'll purr
  for the nonce
  & be stroked.
  Let there be feathers.
  I will not pounce.
1953 Here & gone.
  I'll see them
  at Thanksgiving.
  Troy is fallen.
  The flats are in storage.
1954 Now get you
  to my lady's chamber.
  Make her laugh at that.
  Prithee, Horatio,
  tell me one thing.

OCTOBER 28

We Are Such Stuff

1950 I dream
  I'm in a play
  & haven't
  learned
  my lines.
1951 We were poor
  until the war.
  Then came jobs.
  Moma could put money in the bank
  & buy new teeth.
1952 I reach no climax.
  He disappears two days.
  I go about my business.
  I can wait passive
  as a dune.
1953 My low esteem,
  falling to Herr Brain,
  dragging each night & day,
  even Mr. Bear.
  All's nought.
1954 Why ask Horatio?
  Hamlet at Union.
  Not a tiger
  in the crowd.
  Here's rosemary.

OCTOBER 29

Reversions

1950 Finally
  everyone stands
  staring at me,
  waiting for me to speak
  or the curtain to come down.
1951 The years
  of World War II:
  White Christmases.
  I got a bike
  & ice skates.
1952 I want to waste
  time with Laura & Sybil
  & Lew & Hermes,
  bread baking in the old apartment
  beside Saint Panther's good old days.
1953 All I seemed to need
  from Hermes last weekend
  was news of Sybil & Lew.
  He visits them a little.
  They do not talk of me.
1954 Life is not very important.
  I am imagining New England:
  Hawthorne & Emily Dickinson.
  A village sleeping under trees
  that move in from the woods.

OCTOBER 30

Contagion

1950 How should there not
be ghosts? The planet
engraves
the centuries,
millenia.
1951 Blackouts & rationing
& Hallowe'en. The gang
hanging around the supermarkets,
running to tell Moma
they're selling sugar or coffee.
1952 Letters will have to do.
I write to everyone.
I've heard or read
whenever two bodies touch
the influence continues.
1953 It's taken me
two months
to feel
the smart
of Lew's rejection.
1954 Projected odes:
to Emily Garden,
Nathaniel Haunted House,
& Gertrude Pigeons,
my America.

OCTOBER 31

Haunt

1950 The dead outnumber.
  Rich earth
  is nothing
  but ghosts.
  O Hallowe'en!
1951 The war wasn't bad
  until they dropped
  the bomb.
  I waited
  for mutation.
1952 Friends
  & other
  strangers
  alter
  our cells.
1953 I'm cold
  trying to write a paper
  for Modern British Poets
  with Professor Shields.
  There's no heat in this flat.
1954 He was
  from his mother's
  womb untimely
  ripped: tomorrow
  I'm twenty-one.

NOVEMBER 1

A Birthday Card

1950 I'm seventeen.
  Four years ago
  I won the prize:
  Miss Alice Blue
  in her Hallowe'en guise.
1951 Soon
  I must report
  to be examined
  for the draft:
  "naked to mine enemies."
1952 All souls
  swarm to the trump:
  the dance of death,
  the ship of fools,
  a birthday card.
1953 I think of Alice:
  too big for the door,
  too small to reach the key.
  What are years?
  A rat in a pool of tears.
1954 Bluejay baked a cake for the occasion.
  He's become wonderfully domestic.
  Lilian has made him our family friend.
  How is a cake like a bottle of wine?
  Each in its way is a wheel.

NOVEMBER 2

Someone Stands Silent on the Shore

1950 "The prettiest
girl in the hall!"
The band leader crowed
whipping chiffon
from my boy's bob.
1951 Lady distracts
me at home.
Cirrus resents
my armload of books
under the broken sky.
1952 Bowwow, to celebrate
my birthday suit,
made himself a whale
sounding my seven seas.
Someone stands silent on the shore.
1953 My masks: a fairy's
smirk or youth's
romance or slut's
indifference, philosopher's
stone or weeping child.
1954 Day after day
Lilian clears the way,
sure of herself;
not so sure of me.
But that's no matter.

NOVEMBER 3

"Will You? Won't You? Will You? Won't You?"

1950 But none
of the boys
not even Marty,
would dance with me.
Exquisite solo!
1951 When she is bad
she is horrid: Lady
returns to me
torn & filthy,
probably pregnant.
1952 I am unmoved.
God
help me
I move
unmoved.
1953 Always the same eyes,
apparently my own,
stare back at me.
I do not understand
their blue obliquity.
1954 I begin to meet
the secret strangers
of her former silences:
mostly disapproval,
incomprehension.

NOVEMBER 4

Movies of the Bomb

1950 I remember seventh grade:
movies of the bomb,
my lonely eminence,
& Marty's smart remark,
"Jack measures by the mouthful."
1951 O Laura. We
are such tramps!
"So what have you
to show for it?"
Ambiguous you & we.
1952 Mash & Rex
pack up
& leave
for Argentina.
The party's over.
1953 I have been
born again,
born again,
born again,
until I'd like to die.
1954 She blooms
& I fall.
Her order
bewilders me.
We cross.

NOVEMBER 5

They Are My Father Looking at Me

1950 The novel in my head
   bursts into awareness,
   then burns out again.
   I know it lurks.
   I must go probing.
1951 Lew waits
   for his three hundred dollars
   bail to be
   returned so he
   can take off for Chicago.
1952 Bluejay accuses:
   "How could you let me
   touch you?"
   Dull Jack concludes:
   "You wanted to."
1953 I glance up
   from washing my hands
   & the eyes catch me.
   Simple & hard, they are
   my father looking at me.
1954 We're late for a dinner
   engagement because I'd coaxed
   her into bed as we were dressing.
   She bitches about the sweat
   & inconvenience.

NOVEMBER 6

Scheming

1950 A novel tugs
   the serpent knot
   of people & events,
   taut web of the world's
   dirty silk.
1951 What's in Chicago?
   Some army buddy.
   Lew may not
   leave the state.
   His arrest must come to trial.
1952 "Follow
   your little
   lust. Do just
   what you want.
   Hell? Heaven? The world? can wait."
1953 I'm prone
   to paint myself
   a monster. Maybe
   I'm only bad
   as anybody.
1954 * AA * Ah!
   * BA * Bah!
   * BB * Bees!
   * CAC * Cackle,
   * DD * "Dah-dah!"

NOVEMBER 7

Jack Rattle

1950 The danger is us:
   Sidney & Miss Shrimp,
   Laura & Hermes,
   Sybil & Lew,
   Jack Diamondback.
1951 Christopher Lake,
   a bud I'd like
   to bring to bloom,
   takes dewy sips
   from my scented fingertips.
1952 "Good things
   last. Frustrations
   always pass.
   I am glad
   lust is not easy."
1953 I debase myself
   with Brain & Mr. Bear.
   Still I believe
   my love for Lilian
   is genuine.
1954 * AABABB *
   * CAC * DD *
   I play Pan pipes, perhaps a lyre,
   in the formal garden
   among the fireflies. Or are they stars?

NOVEMBER 8

Bulls

1950 Miss Shrimp
opposes Sidney,
Sidney opposes
Miss Shrimp.
Atheist & Catholic.
1951 Laura
may scare him away.
Chris cross!
Her intensity
bullies.
1952 Hermes' mother
called me Wednesday.
Theresa is tubercular
& must leave college
for a year.
1953 I remain determined
to put everything down.
Keep your books
in order
& let matters run.
1954 "To die of a rose
in aromatic bliss,"
Pope proclaims folly.
With Keats I sniff
the Fernando passion.

NOVEMBER 9

A Score

1950 Laura (in the novel Maryann)
mews curiosity. Whoever
would lead her astray,
her parents or me,
she perfects butterfly.
1951 Lew insists logic
explains our behavior.
Should I divine
what his brooding harbors
he'd call me invalid.
1952 That's a story
she's been told to spare
her feelings. I hear
from Hermes in a letter
the less pleasant score.
1953 Lilian & I have most
of our classes together.
I doze through the day,
drooping over books,
dreaming in her lap.
1954 Pope's bone.
Keats' flesh.
Milton's intellect.
Chaucer's warm soul.
Shakespeare's dark.

NOVEMBER 10

Sad Distances

1950 Hermes (call him Saul):
wit's clippership,
moon schooner,
fancy's poop deck
& raw sail.
1951 Ugliness decays
& debauches me.
Beauty recalls
& burdens me with time.
Some distances grow sad.
1952 Theresa depressed
sought a psychiatrist.
He ticked off the minutiae of guilt:
she's left the church & loved a Jew
& lied to her family.
1953 I talked to Dixie.
I have to be honest with someone.
Herr Brain & Mr. Bear & Lew & Lilian.
"It's certainly
a mess," she said.
1954 Hawthorne's guilt
& Whitman's glory,
Emily's bitchery
& Stein's integrity
quicken the heir.

NOVEMBER 11

The Flexible Spine

1950 The novel will be real
like a dew
& the deep sea.
People trying to live their dreams
intrude on the dreams of other people.
1951 Walked home with Chris
& gained his confidence.
He has said no
to a plague of moths
but still burns.
1952 She told her mother all
about Hermes & her fall.
Her mother abducted her:
a doctor, a priest,
& Arizona.
1953 Lilian deserves
fidelity. How
may I lash her
to my perilous
androgyny?
1954 Rhyme shimmers, the flexible spine
that supports the brain.
The stung hand snakes
the pen across paper,
an invention of bees.

NOVEMBER 12

Hot Little Hands

1950 A novel sweats rude
  as best people do.
  I must find the tangle
  of events that drives each person
  toward entanglement: a plot.
1951 I have great plans
  for Christopher.
  Beginning balls vague
  but inciting: the clay
  in my hot little hands.
1952 This rigamarole
  of tubercule
  & conscience
  is simple
  antisemitism.
1953 Need fawns not enough.
  Love crows not enough.
  Happiness bloats not enough.
  Poses, Lilian, poses.
  The truth won't do.
1954 Saint Sartre says,
  "Man is a useless passion"
  & "Hell is other people."
  Saint Mephistopheles:"Myself am hell
  and hell is where I am."

NOVEMBER 13

Nobody's Home

1950 Will anyone survive?
Laura perhaps.
She'll waft
on silent wings
beyond the net of words.
1951 America's retarded adolescence,
epoch of terrible fear,
forgetful of the free
child in the apple tree.
Nobody's home.
1952 I think of the puritan
& unnecessary exhumation
of Camille in Dumas' novel.
Morality requires
humiliation exceeding the grave.
1953 What is truth?
It is not the man
who stands before you.
I weary
of fooling myself.
1954 Useless,
I need no one to point the way.
Here's only the beginning of our misery.
"The mind is its own place
and in itself can make. . ."

NOVEMBER 14

Benvenuto in the Pope's Tower

1950 I call my novel
The Misunderstood
because it is people:
we are essentially
mistaken.
1951 Best known phrases gape emptiest.
We take memory for comprehension.
Nearest people loom strangest.
We take proximity for understanding.
Familiarity breeds ignorance.
1952 Love
like Benvenuto
in the pope's tower
will find
its way.
1953 How do I rejoice
in this claptrap?
I am in love
with love's
absurdity.
1954 Let there be no misunderstanding.
I have loved no one; no one has loved me.
This is not extraordinary but the common lot.
The world is not made
of love, by love, for love.

NOVEMBER 15

Most Irregular

1950 Could digression
& distraction be
a method?
Life mainly disports,
but have I art enough?
1951 Creation manifests inequalities.
Nature bounds most
irregular & without
fear. O! "The world
is so full. . ."
1952 Bluejay won't
speak to me & seems
self-satisfied about it.
I choose to love
a miserable nonsense.
1953 Lilian confessed,
& straight-faced too,
that Bluejay attempted to seduce her
& she submitted to some tentative caresses.
I laughed. I couldn't help myself.
1954 Having graduated last June,
Dixie now teaches English
at an American college
in Turkey. She writes
from Istanbul.

NOVEMBER 16

Apparitions

1950 An apparition,
  I fade among a mire
  of souls, untouched
  by the world's traffic,
  insubstantial.
1951 Christopher keeps
  a list of numbers
  which he regularly calls:
  intimate conversations with strangers
  who do not know his name.
1952 I still
  believe
  in sin,
  suicide,
  & boredom.
1953 She walked out furious.
  Now we have had a long confessional.
  I left out Mr. Bear & Brain.
  We admitted our doubts
  & tenderness returned.
1954 "You're a breath of fresh air."
  What they create
  with their cliches!
  If we are fresh air,
  the world is in trouble.

NOVEMBER 17

Making Holes

1950 What is wrong
with chasing bugs?
Miss Shrimp
nets a last word.
Laura stands silent with pins.
1951 I am reminded
of the man
who buys dreams
in Truman Capote's
Master Misery.
1952 A bore
is a tool
to make holes.
I have taken
several lovers.
1953 Lilian arrived
with records
& we spent
a lovely day
studying to Debussy.
1954 Our future maps out:
graduate school,
professorships,
perhaps a child
when she is ready.

NOVEMBER 18

Wing & Worm

1950 The wing
  & the worm:
  the novel
  must live
  so we can.
1951 A pomp of pansies!
  When righteous boys
  mistake their latency
  for virtue, I want
  to sit on their faces.
1952 Theresa's letter
  refracts the view:
  she really has a lung
  infection & anemia. Her mother
  is close to a nervous collapse.
1953 People say
  you cannot change the past.
  I find it a different place
  each time I visit.
  Nothing stands fixed.
1954 No poetry infects her plan.
  I notice that she does not notice this.
  She likes to have me read my poems to company,
  but when I want to work,
  there's work to do.

NOVEMBER 19

Snowman

1950 The novel must have art so it will live.
 What kind of theme:
 indefinition?
 What sort of story:
 abstraction?
1951 Ecstacy shattered
 body & mind & mouth
 to utterance.
 In the beginning
 language. . .
1952 My long walk
 fogged the night.
 I made the night unreel
 leering at infrequent strangers:
 I have a secret you would love to know.
1953 Proteus
 simply performs
 his metamorphoses
 while I hold on wheeling,
 kicking stars out of their orbits.
1954 "This evening children in the street have run
 out of their mittens making lovely men
 of snow. From odds and ends of coal a stare
 and grin that little hands leave guardian
 exclude our praise surrendering to prayer."

Saints & Sinners

1950 My name
  will be Morris.
  I want to call
  myself a name.
  Everyone has.
1951 I must violate
  good taste,
  stand artless,
  risk misunderstanding.
  Otherwise I cannot hope.
1952 I have a secret I would love to know.
  I played Tchaikovsky on my wrists again
  with Grampa's razor.
  I bore myself a lot.
  A trifle of sinners.
1953 A weekend in Huntington & Brooklyn.
  Henry J's on blocks for the winter.
  I spent a night in Mr. Bear's smart cave.
  Hibernation might suffice.
  Then I could wake to lilies.
1954 "Hello, Miss Stein. And when you left your chair
  beside the fire, walking in the snow
  you made discovery of prayer for fun
  that once upon a time. Hello, hello,
  Miss Stein, hello: the variations fall."

NOVEMBER 21

The Morris

1950 It's a men's
  folk dance
  celebrating spring
  or harvest, trying
  to get earth pregnant.
1951 My contradictions
  are too well controlled.
  Gide's *Lafcadio*
  validates my terror
  of labels.
1952 Woo
  & then wound
  is Bluejay's way.
  Thank God
  for a rainy season.
1953 Herr Brain
  for his aberrance
  continues
  my amusing
  courtier.
1954 "Miss Stein, hello: the variations fall
  into the snow as you repeat them all."
  A quickness of imps & angels spins my clay.
  The first stanza of *Walking in Snow* is done.
  Yes, it will do.

NOVEMBER 22

Looking for God

1950 Morris flees the church.
He goes looking for God
in the hailstone,
hillside,
dew.
1951 Desire
frequently
prevents
its own
fulfillment.
1952 Rain calls me out.
I've covered Albany
forgetting classes,
forgetting friends.
The wet is bittersweet.
1953 Today for instance
he stopped his lecture
at lunch to admire
the grace, the wounded-wing
fall of my hands in repose.
1954 If the stanza has eleven lines
the poem must have eleven stanzas.
I do not understand my own arithmetic
but "Number is ecstacy,"
said Baudelaire.

NOVEMBER 23

Baptisms

1950 I had to hate the church
before God could be real
as Grandmother Raven's
conchshell, easy to hear,
impossible to know.
1951 I will no longer struggle.
Let it come down.
I want only to be alone
on some island of stone
& evergreen.
1952 The rain baptizes.
Everything is sacrament.
Soaked sneakers
slap like aspergilium
the aspergory streets.
1953 He's equally apt
to leer while I peel
a banana. "It's a strip
tease," says he, & winces
as I sink my sexy teeth.
1954 Five sections make an ode:
apostrophe, description, celebration.
Personal digression: really an assimilation.
A gradual disintegration
of our two identities.

NOVEMBER 24

The Body is Not Important

1950 The body is not important
  Morris thinks.
  Does Morris think
  the body is not important?
  He makes it his excuse.
1951 I wish I were a dancer
  or a painter
  or a pianist.
  I wish I were anything but a poet.
  I am not a dancer, painter, pianist, or poet.
1952 Bluejay gave me an old paperback
  of Isherwood's *Mr. Norris*. A newspaper
  clipping fell from its pages about his older
  sister's graduation & her college activities,
  memberships, awards. I cried.
1953 This flat won't do.
  The roaches dominate
  the kitchen & my brain.
  It's odd that once you've seen the first
  they suddenly swarm. Everywhere like God.
1954 "The children in the street know how to play."
  Hermes has forgotten me.
  I'm treading a white balloon
  not hearing from him.
  I wish we had a phone.

NOVEMBER 25

Thanksgivings

1950 I wrote a first chapter
of *The Misunderstood*:
Morris & Maryann
playing with insects
in a wood.
1951 Rasputin tied up circulation
calling old friends all evening
from County P inviting them
to join him in a mass
suicide party.
1952 Beats me
why I cried.
Nothing could
have been
more ordinary.
1953 Hecuba cannot be dissuaded
the landlord's bed is her box.
His old dog too has fits
of diarrhea which she can't control.
I'm cleaning up a lot of shit.
1954 In September we came home
to bags of groceries
from Moma at the downstairs door.
We didn't hear from them again.
We wrote inviting them for Thanksgiving.

NOVEMBER 26

A Damned Nuisance

1950 I am not ready.
The seed revolves
in my mind
like a penny
trying to be the sun.
1951 Tanner put a stop to Rasputin.
She didn't think him funny.
She didn't think him sad.
Simply a damned nuisance & bad
for business.
1952 I woke feeling sure
the world had ended
while I slept.
Each normal event
confirmed my feeling.
1953 Give over.
My hair
has gone
quite gold.
I love disorder.
1954 My father
fell in
to a coma.
Came out
diabetic.

NOVEMBER 27

Tchaikovsky & Frank Sinatra

1950 I moon over Welkin.
  Tchaikovsky
  & Frank Sinatra.
  Drop into bed so early
  even Moma is alarmed.
1951 Violence & squalor
  everybody loves.
  I prefer beauty.
  There's more
  terror in it.
1952 Thanksgiving
  with Sybil & Lew.
  I say I am in love
  as if it were
  a simple story.
1953 Beans:
  beans:
  beans:
  the gods
  are beans.
1954 Moma weighs
  all his food.
  He's slim as a boy.
  Even Lilian enjoyed
  his company.

NOVEMBER 28

I Smile Prettily

1950 Morris will be strangled
in a stalled elevator
by an enraged pervert.
Maryann will come
to no conclusion.
1951 Somewhere I read
"New York ain't America."
Divine & indifferent city.
Everything is there.
But I am here.
1952 Lew pranced & petted
boyish in his glee.
He crowed at me
of love & doodle-do.
I smiled prettily.
1953 A freshman girl
has joined our party.
Her name is Vera Freund.
I shall no longer worry
about the names.
1954 I remember
when Dad
drove a truck
delivering beer
to bars & barracks.

NOVEMBER 29

Against the Sky

1950 Welkin will tumble
across my bright board,
solitary & unaware
as some red checker.
Maybe he will strangle Morris.
1951 The city,
Hermes,
the ballet,
& Jose Greco's
Spanish whip.
1952 Hermes came to breakfast.
The landlady, Mrs. Cross,
was drunk at ten o'clock.
We were sober.
Even Lew.
1953 I'll skin
Mr. Bear.
I'm cold
& do not care
a bean.
1954 Big Dad,
big truck,
& little Jack.
Childhood is
forever.

NOVEMBER 30

Floating Away

1950 Laura & I
sat on the steps
at County P
wishing we were balloons
to float away.
1951 On the train
I mused impressed
by vegetable nature
covering the scars
men have inflicted.
1952 Mrs. Cross
bored us with labels.
Lew is intelligent,
Hermes talented,
I am the beautiful one.
1953 I refused
to waste the night
with Herr Brain.
"You do not suffer.
It shows in your poems," said he.
1954 I do remember snow
higher than my seven-league galoshes
& a room full of young
men in uniform making
much over little Jack Horn.

DECEMBER 1

I Think It's a Dirty Joke

1950 Some cars
shed crepe paper
passing the house,
just married,
a horny racket.
1951 Following Hermes
I slough my basilisk.
Today I went to work,
sat by the river,
ate my dinner.
1952 Jack
springs eternal,
the beautiful one.
I can hear Laura saying,
"I think it's a dirty joke."
1953 I passify Herr Brain.
He wants me there
at dawn, naked
in his blue kimono,
paisley & second hand.
1954 It's good
to know Dad
& I shared
a trucker's cab
one winter.

DECEMBER 2

Begin with Silence

1950 I sold my ass
  for ice cream.
  I was nine.
  I'm seventeen.
  I want to seduce the sky.
1951 A movie begins
  with silence except
  the swish of a needle.
  The dark screen flashes
  taking our picture.
1952 "You are
  my wholeness,"
  sang Bluejay
  splitting peas
  & hairs & atoms.
1953 Besides her diarrhea
  the landlord's dog
  has just the dumb
  face that makes me
  numb with rage.
1954 Moma will tell you
  I didn't talk
  till I was four.
  I had the good sense
  then.

DECEMBER 3

Behind Snowmen's Eyes

1950 Welkin sat alone
in his classroom reading.
I stood out
of sight in the hall
watching.
1951 Christopher wept
& then fell
asleep while I held
his cold hand. He doesn't
know which way to go.
1952 The vulgar spirit
makes the sky
a cage.
Birdsong.
Birdseed.
1953 Attar
of roses.
Nobody
wants to hurt
anybody.
1954 "Know how to play,
know how to pack
the falling snow away
behind the snowmen's eyes."
Ancient fires lurk.

DECEMBER 4

Looming at Galaxies

1950 His name
  roars
  & rips.
  He is the sky.
  I am the rain.
1951 I didn't think
  it mattered much
  which way one went.
  The whole thing
  is to go.
1952 Bowwow
  performs
  his tricks
  in a lace
  collar.
1953 I searched
  & found a grim shop
  where I could cradle a cup
  of black coffee
  alone.
1954 As I approach some mastery of craft
  I apprehend the promised end of art.
  Terrifying freedom
  opens at my feet.
  I loom at galaxies.

DECEMBER 5

A Child is Born

1950 I have seen boys
  wag like puppies
  for each other
  & nobody called
  them queer.
1951 I must fly
  my kite or we
  will end up
  hanging in a tree.
  Paper & string.
1952 I should sing
  bareback
  on a pony
  round & round
  the golden ring.
1953 I've gone
  into hiding.
  Anybody
  mobs me
  out of mind.
1954 A child is born.
  A girl: Lo! Belle.
  Hermes calls us
  through the school.
  The first snow fell.

DECEMBER 6

The Full Heart

1950 I sat among
  an audience
  high strung
  beneath a bow
  & fingertips.
1951 I want
  to throw
  my rider
  & run wild
  down defile.
1952 "Pony Girl,
  Pony Girl,
  won't you
  be my pony.
  Girl?"
1953 "The soul selects
  her own society.
  Then shuts the door."
  Weeds choke me
  out of soil.
1954 Hermes has a daughter.
  Miriam, I'm drunk
  on the communion wine.
  "My heart is full
  of longing after snow."

DECEMBER 7

Spells

1950 I will keep my temper
with Lew & English teachers.
Now I know
spelling
is important.
1951 Night
mares:
Mary:
mere:
la mer.
1952 The spot
light spills.
In shadow
neither black nor brilliant
sits the audience.
1953 I wish I were Keats'
Adonis sleeping
or anemone
beneath the sea's
slow steeping.
1954 Work pulls me together.
Words are snowfall
cooling my fever.
Lust & disfavor
fade before endeavor.

DECEMBER 8

Myself the Bait

1950 Even *Death in Venice*
  I am reading now
  sings only alphabet.
  The look & listen in the letter
  lures me, myself the bait.
1951 I should not kill
  me: I am not mine.
  I learned my catechism well.
  The great art is allow
  death to come like cockcrow.
1952 Black
  & brilliant
  I watch
  my audience
  watch me.
1953 I find new hiding places every day
  & try to make peace by writing
  poems to my friends.
  Their absence
  doesn't squander me.
1954 "How can we know,
  how can the snow be vast,
  how can the sky be vast:
  how can we know it is snowing,
  how can we know the snow?"

DECEMBER 9

The Word Is There

1950 Alpha!
  Omega!
  What is
  the universe?
  First Tooth.
1951 Emily knew.
  Play dead.
  The flies & gentlemen
  will come to you.
  I lean against the sun.
1952 I should have listened
  to the world,
  my little friends
  who called me every name
  except my own.
1953 I trust
  my spirit
  to endure.
  The word
  is there.
1954 "My words exclude another's eyes: my flesh
  is commonplace, or seems, like snow: my ghost
  remains the gift of prayer and puzzle. . .
  Words make visible the world, the rhyme,
  the measure of its harmony and form."

DECEMBER 10

Tangle

1950 Each day
  I write
  a chapter,
  tear it up
  unread.
1951 How fine
  once to awaken
  & discover
  at one's pillow
  morning!
1952 Life slobbers, big
  unwelcomed dog,
  all tongue & tail,
  never a neat
  beginning & no end.
1953 A tryptych for Hermes.
  In three couplets I try
  to give him Cimabue,
  Botticelli,
  & Van Gogh.
1954 Talk
  about poetry.
  Don't tell.
  Don't tell me
  there's no jack in it.

DECEMBER 11

The Stars Whisper

1950 Hermes scornful,
  Laura panting
  to the rescue:
  "Are you mad?"
  Lew understands.
1951 To be born.
  How was I snatched
  into the world
  that I need
  to be born?
1952 I'm rafting after Twain
  discovering my brain
  is Tom, my heart
  is Huck. Jim is my soul
  & my body is the river.
1953 Christ
  & the goddess
  & the stars
  whisper.
  We must attend them, Hermes.
1954 Nothing disturbs me
  but anticipation
  of the journey
  to Brooklyn.
  Ecce puella!

DECEMBER 12

A Pretty Thing

1950 Laura wants a compact:
   enamel & filigree
   with powder & a mirror.
   A pretty thing like proms
   she invents to mock me.
1951 What means it
   to be new?
   What is a rose
   but the fancy
   of some old root?
1952 *Huck Finn,*
   The Scarlet Letter.
   I retreat into the somber art
   of Hawthorne & the crafty
   imperfections of Mark Twain.
1953 For Lilian I've written
   about damselflies
   how the male
   lifts the female free
   of the water's breaking tension.
1954 Hermes,
   "we take
   the weather
   in our arms
   like song."

DECEMBER 13

The Cookie House

1950 For Sybil I found
   a web of wafting silk,
   hand-painted roses'
   translucence,
   lunacy.
1951 I'd want to be
   outside the universe.
   Hamlet's despondency,
   Dad's banality: "Seen one?
   You've seen them all."
1952 Living wastes me.
   Birds & bowwows raise
   a too familiar noise
   that ruptures ears.
   I rapture myself in books.
1953 Soon I will go
   with Lilian to share
   a German Christmas.
   Hansel und Gretel
   seek the cookie house.
1954 Two weeks ago
   a suffocating stench
   filled the livingroom.
   I thought it was me
   in the sea's old womb.

DECEMBER 14

Involution

1950 Lew despises
every poem I bring,
each tune I sing.
"Cliche!
Cliche!"
1951 I was reared
on that dull motto
like a turd.
Process is princess
& involution is her lord.
1952 I stand forever cold
at midnight, cold at dawn,
waiting for the bus.
Schenectady to Albany:
Albany to Schenectady.
1953 We will enact
der Kinder
for a week.
Long Island.
Let it snow.
1954 A rat
died in the walls.
No scrubbing
could absolve
his rot.

DECEMBER 15

Carols

1950 I should not write
for him or anyone.
I should not write.
Why is this drizzle
& not snow?
1951 My head aches.
The light dances,
shimmering amoebas.
My heart waits
for Hermes.
1952 Rosemary Clooney
croons in the corner.
"Hey there you
with the stars
in your eyes."
1953 I gathered Lilian.
Hand in hand
we descended
downtown to get lost
among crowds & carols.
1954 The reek outlasted days.
Then a fire ravaged
the house next door.
Now waterbugs infest
our sodden nest.

DECEMBER 16

Snow Queen

1950 I would chase snowflakes
   with Laura. She will frame them
  . like her butterflies.
   She could do it.
   But it doesn't snow.
1951 Every sentence compromises.
   Will I ever write well?
   I want detachment.
   Every word is death
   by drowning or conflagration.
1952 I'm melting the frost
   off my bedroom window.
   Each fingertip absorbs
   a tiny forest.
   Snow Queen!
1953 We had dinner
   & stayed out until her curfew.
   Through frost-misted lashes
   we could see each other's
   moon wings.
1954 We chase them
   with Raid or Flit.
   They are so fat
   we sicken at the thought,
   crushing them underfoot.

DECEMBER 17

Romona Lurks Below

1950 I blew a week's pay
buying a pipe for Lew.
Black stem & ivory bowl
to frame the dark aroma
of his vanilla leaf.
1951 Sometimes we ask
too much of verbs.
I weary of the hunt.
Hermes wings his big feet
northward while I sleep.
1952 Hot Fudge
sends sketches.
Only a cat
can lick ass
like saving grace.
1953 Lilian does not share
my view that women are
superior. She assures me
that female
means petty.
1954 Romona
lurks
below us
& controls
the thermostat.

DECEMBER 18

A Funny Word

1950 Sybil leaves
   to visit parents.
   God knows
   where Lew is off to.
   Saranac?
1951 Christopher says, "Friend."
   It's such a funny word:
   in Germany almost *happiness,*
   in French so nearly *soul,*
   in English little more than *fiend.*
1952 The cat's
   weird eyes
   express
   the serpent core
   of seraphim.
1953 She told me about former beaux.
   I guess that only one
   made any real
   impression on her spirit
   & she lost him to the priesthood.
1954 Romona likes it hot.
   I'm sent down
   to complain. Lilian
   roars down
   looming above.

DECEMBER 19

Rose & Almond

1950 On Friday
 Lew prepared a feast.
 Port & Burgundy to float the salads,
 cookies flavored rose & almond,
 cashews & hot buttered rum.
1951 Between
 F & D:
 rien.
 Between you & me
 that's *nothing.*
1952 Bluejay surprised me
 (& Moma more)
 knocking at her kitchen door.
 Wouldn't he come
 the back way!
1953 I'd make her
 my church,
 my altar,
 my communion
 supper.
1954 Hag rage made hell
 of the dove's nest.
 Now burns low.
 The phoenix
 had no mate.

DECEMBER 20

Closeted

1950 The three of us at table
  by candlelight
  steal by night
  into some pharaoh tomb or still
  more ancient burial.
1951 Hermes hardly reached home
  & we were closeted in his room
  with music. I told him all
  about my day
  at the induction center.
1952 We went to see
  Lana Turner (*The Bad
  and the Beautiful*).
  Spent the night
  in my lisping bed.
1953 Poppa Trout
  hauls in the *Tannenbaum*.
  Wonderful food & drink
  flow from the kitchen
  into my dreams.
1954 We have to keep our windows
  open against the heat.
  I sit & write.
  Lilian assumes
  my quietude is spite.

DECEMBER 21

An Opening of Graves

1950 We are an opening of graves.
  We tore into our presents.
  They gave me Mozart
  & a Playtex
  girdle.
1951 My first is firehouse.
  We gathered to be bused
  to Albany for testing.
  "Are you attracted
  to members of your sex?"
1952 He promises
  to stay with me
  in Brooklyn.
  I promise Lew
  & Sybil.
1953 Hospitality
  restores me.
  I am included
  in family usages.
  They speak to me in German.
1954 Let there be noise.
  I sit in the heat
  & write about snow,
  the snowflake silence
  of the houseled word.

DECEMBER 22

I Am Able to Fill a Blank

1950 Then Lew announced
  he was leaving,
  had an appointment.
  Sybil fell silent.
  He slammed out.
1951 "I adore
  the members
  of my sex."
  I am able
  to fill a blank.
1952 Hermes arrives
  two days before I leave.
  I'm glad he misses Bluejay.
  He plays me new Stravinsky.
  We talk only about the music.
1953 Sometimes I understand
  as if I knew the language.
  Some mad king long ago
  built castles on the Rhine.
  Maybe I learned German on his knee.
1954 Poetry sounds the divine madness
  that dances me along the line
  of scarce balance. The poem
  is the work that must be done
  to keep me clean.

DECEMBER 23

Fever

1950 Candlelight,
   jazz from the radio,
   glasses & plates,
   her tears,
   the glitter.
1951 I camped
   & schoolmates,
   naked, knew
   what I was up to.
   They did not jeer.
1952 At last he says
   he has not heard from Theresa,
   does not know where she is.
   Hermes & I talk.
   We never touch.
1953 Moma Trout comes home
   from market & says *Jew*.
   I have to hold my tongue.
   I look toward Lilian.
   She unpacks the groceries.
1954 We were to take a train
   this morning to Long Island.
   Lilian is down
   with fever.
   She can only sleep.

DECEMBER 24

Birds in a Chimney

1950 He returned.
  He stormed: he would
  not have servility.
  I know how birds
  fret baffled in a chimney.
1951 They add some chemical
  to our urine.
  The specimen
  turns blue.
  "How pretty!"
1952 I arrive
  for Christmas Eve.
  They give me
  Ronald Firbanks
  & Lew's good meal.
1953 We toast
  the fatherland at 6:00 PM,
  midnight in Germany.
  "O little town
  of Bethlehem."
1954 We find a doctor
  who gives her an injection
  & pills. The trains are all
  late: crowded & hot. We fall
  into the arms of Poppa Trout.

DECEMBER 25

A Christmas Card

1950 Christ! The world
  is a battlefield.
  I read folktales
  & poems of Korea.
  The war is a war.
1951 A farmboy
  in the line up
  for the blood test
  passed out. Scarecrow
  flubs the rubber floor.
1952 All is well.
  Lew's very excited
  about Kierkegaard
  & Bluejay. Sybil
  hands me a bough.
1953 On Christmas day
  in the morning
  Lilian drives me
  to a lonely bay
  of sea & sky & gull.
1954 Lilian will
  only sleep
  & take pills
  until Moma Trout
  loses her temper.

DECEMBER 26

Pictures of the Wounded

1950 I look in *Life*
at pictures of the wounded.
They are what I expected.
It requires no imagination
to know war.
1951 At last
I was sent
to the psychiatrist.
"Have you ever been
cornholed?"
1952 I showed Lew
my few poems.
He ripped
me apart
of course.
1953 We've settled down
to writing term papers
on the diningroom table.
She does the Medici.
I do Thomas More.
1954 I traveled alone
to Brooklyn to see
the Christmas child.
O Hermes! O Miriam!
"Has she any wool?"

DECEMBER 27

My Good News

1950 Moma insisted I accompany her to church
on Christmas. She wants to save my soul.
The church & the war are the same.
They maim & impoverish the spirit
& the flesh. For someone's profit.

1951 An inquisition.
I answered growling
like a dog
or bellows
of my bowels.

1952 Bluejay arrived last night.
The three of us were very gay
this morning. Sybil slept late.
We brought her breakfast on a tray.
Whence this brief epoch of our levity?

1953 Mr. Bear hosts
a party in Brooklyn.
Hermes & Hot Fudge
& lots of people
we don't know.

1954 Lilian was better
when I returned
but I tired her
with my good news.
I wait to tell her more.

DECEMBER 28

Le Dernier Cri

1950 If God is everywhere
he's in the church & war.
I suppose he is even
in someone's profit.
All is too much for me.
1951 I listen
to Judith Anderson's
Medea. That couple
is so middle class.
Dead boys. Dead boys.
1952 We are all
playing awhile
that life
is love's
young dream.
1953 We hang around
Mr. Bear's apartment
waiting for New Year's Eve,
listening to Eartha Kitt
& *Gentlemen Prefer Blondes.*
1954 "Days pass: the world turns on itself like snow.
This is the most exclusive prayer I know."
I finished the ode while Lilian slept in her fever,
took it to Crumb's stag party looking for Chum
who is a listener, got drunk & seduced the groom.

DECEMBER 29

Herr Brain Walks in to Mock

1950 "I am the one who dies
when he is not loved,"
wrote Nijinsky in his *Diary*.
Laura gave me Nijinsky
& Isadora Duncan.
1951 In my dream I looked down
on a high & terrible stone wall.
On one side stood downcast
an utterly dejected man,
empty & idle.
1952 Meanwhile I'm trying
to read Kierkegaard
which Lew thrusts into my lap
while he stews or plays Chopin
on their new piano.
1953 Hot Fudge
had us round to dinner.
Mr. Bear & Lilian & Hermes.
Then Sybil arrived
with Lew.
1954 The guests had left but Herr Brain
walked in to mock us.
At dawn in a diner
he absolved me saying,
"I envy your humiliation."

DECEMBER 30

Conclusions

1950 Moma
  will never
  understand
  I am her
  rage & fear.
1951 I saw myself walking
  & the poor man's wife
  came to me complaining
  of his worthlessness
  & her great love.
1952 When I get home
  there will surely be
  a note for me
  from Bluejay
  saying *boohoo*.
1953 This was Hermes'
  doing. Life is
  going very right
  & very wrong.
  We have a full cast.
1954 The child lives.
  I only know
  the child lives
  & the rest
  is not important.

DECEMBER 31

In Which Nothing is Concluded

1950 Bean, stalk.
   Beans talk.
   My head balks
   all a scattering
   of shadows.
1951 I said she was a barren woman
   or she would fold her man
   into her flesh & give him life.
   I woke up wondering
   where dreams are born.
1952 Midnight: I stood
   on the roof with Lew
   & we looked over the city.
   "AESTHETIC, MORAL, SPIRITUAL."
   It was very cold.
1953 Whatever
   finds
   form
   takes
   fire.
1954 *Beans* sown
   at Samos, Walden Pond,
   Lake Isle of Innisfree,
   Crooked Hill Road, Long Island.
   "Uncle! Uncle!"

About the Author

The author, Tom Smith, at age 17 and at age 70.

TOM SMITH is Professor Emeritus at Castleton State College in Vermont. He has been publishing poetry since 1959, and is the author of several books, including *Waiting on Pentecost*, published by Birch Brook Press. He is married to soprano and actress Virginia DeAngelis Smith; they have two grown sons, four grandsons, and one granddaughter.